STEWARDSHIP
IN MISSION

LIBRARY OF CHRISTIAN STEWARDSHIP

AUTHORS

Elmer J. F. Arndt is Professor of Systematic Theology, Eden Theological Seminary, Webster Groves, Missouri.

Roger Hazelton is Dean of the Oberlin Graduate School of Theology, Oberlin, Ohio.

Frederick Herzog is Professor of Systematic Theology, Duke University, Durham, North Carolina.

Ralph D. Hyslop is Professor of Church History, Union Theological Seminary, New York, New York.

Roy Pearson is Dean of the Andover Newton Theological School, Newton Center, Massachusetts.

Winburn T. Thomas is Secretary of the Department of Interpretation and Stewardship, General Council, United Presbyterian Church, U.S.A., New York, New York.

T. K. Thompson is Executive Director of the Department of Stewardship and Benevolence of the National Council of the Churches of Christ in the U.S.A., New York, New York.

Hugh Vernon White is Dean Emeritus of Pacific School of Religion, Berkeley, California.

STEWARDSHIP
IN MISSION

by
Winburn T. Thomas

Prentice-Hall, Inc., Englewood Cliffs, N.J.

Library of Congress Catalog Card Number: 64-20978
Printed in the United States of America
T 84658 (paper)   T 84656 (case)

Prentice-Hall International, Inc., *London*
Prentice-Hall of Australia, Pty., Ltd., *Sydney*
Prentice-Hall of Canada, Ltd., *Toronto*
Prentice-Hall of India (Private) Ltd., *New Delhi*
Prentice-Hall of Japan, Inc., *Tokyo*
Prentice-Hall de Mexico, S. A., *Mexico City*

CONTENTS

INTRODUCTION

LIBRARY OF CHRISTIAN STEWARDSHIP is designed to help pastors and stewardship-finance leaders of congregations with needed background materials. Volume one, *Handbook of Stewardship Procedures*, affords a basic outline of the full range of Christian stewardship. Included are important source references to books, films, filmstrips and denominational literature. The companion volume, *Stewardship in Mission*, is a symposium edited by Winburn T. Thomas. The central theme elaborated by respected theologians affirms that Christian stewardship must issue in a vigorous missionary activity and that mission must be based on principles of stewardship. Forthcoming volumes will consider: the Christian Meaning of Money, Stewardship Illustrations, a Stewardship Commentary on the Old Testament, a Stewardship Commentary on the New Testament—and related themes.

All volumes in the series will be published both in cloth and paperback editions. Their convenient size, attractive format and reasonable price will enable the local church to obtain multiple copies for use in leadership training, group study and program development. The contributors will be recognized authorities in the subject area treated. Popularly written, each book will serve as a reliable guide and ready reference for key leaders in the congregation.

T. K. THOMPSON
General Editor

PREFACE

Winburn T. Thomas

"It is the commonplace of our time that we are living in an age of skepticism. How shall we meet it? We are living in an age of spiritual apathy. How shall we arouse the church? We are living in an age that has no revivals. How shall we bring back the days of Whitfield?" [1] Thus Rev. Lyman Abbott addressed the Haystack Centennial Meeting of the American Board in 1906. These questions are being asked even more sharply today, and the answers have become more difficult. This symposium on Stewardship and Mission is offered in the hope that its message may help arouse the churches from their lethargy and stimulate them to renewed activity. In their original form all but the concluding essay were speeches delivered in a series of conferences across the nation. Addressed to the theme, "Stewardship and Mission," they evidence a considerable departure from earlier notions of "benevolence" and "missions." While there are points of overlapping, and the theological and sociological thrust are within the same tradition, each makes a distinctive contribution to the church's understanding of its larger mission and to the place of the Christian within Christ's expectations.

[1] Minutes of the 97th Annual Meeting of the American Board, ABCFM, (Boston, 1907) p. 264.

Christendom in our day has rediscovered the relevancy of the Bible; it is being reformed and renewed by ecumenical developments; it is moving from the limited confines of "missions" to the large "mission" involvement of the church in the world; it is reinterpreting the "ministry" in the Pauline sense of each Christian being endowed with gifts of the Holy Spirit which are to be employed for the perfecting of the saints; and it has defined stewardship to include the responsible use by Christians of all they are and have in the work of Christ's kingdom.

The reader will note a blurring in the use of terms. Stewardship, mission, discipleship, witness, service, and evangelism may be used by the different writers to indicate similar or different ideas. As to the broad definition of stewardship, each probably would subscribe to this formulation, as suggested by Rev. Hans-Ruedi Weber, the Associate Director of the Ecumenical Institute in Switzerland:

> We are stewards of God because all we are, and have, and live has been entrusted to us by God, so that we may glorify Him. This implies that our stewardship concerns basically not only our possessions, but also our whole being and the universe we live in. And it implies that this stewardship is asked from us in the world of our daily work, our houses, and leisure-time activities, as well as for the corporate worship and work of the church.[2]

None of the writers limits the use of the term to apply only to participation in organized church activities or assumes that God's work is especially confined to what happens in and through the church. Generally, they assume that stewardship is also applicable to secular work, politics, race relations, the outlawry of war, etc., as well as to the use of time, abilities, and money, evangelism, etc.

The major emphasis, however, is upon the theological basis of stewardship and mission, and it is at this point that the articles are of prime value to the pastor. The editor does not subscribe to the idea that there is a "theology of stewardship" or

[2] *Christian Stewardship and Ecumenical Confrontation*, Department of Stewardship and Benevolence, NCCUSA (New York, 1961) pp. 8-9.

a separate "theology of mission." Rather, he is of the conviction that within theology there are stewardship and mission dimensions, and the contributors do, in fact, write according to this understanding.

While the stewardship movement was started to provide support for the missionary outreach of the church, says Thomas K. Thompson,[3] Roger Hazleton and Elmer J. F. Arndt posit it on gratitude, the thankful witness for God's benevolence in his gift of Christ to the world, and say it is the expression of our obedience in mission. Roy Pearson interprets stewardship as "the essential status of man in his wholeness . . ." and missions as "stewardship in action." The theology of these two is "the study of God's relationship to his property." Hugh Vernon White discusses stewardship in terms of its Greek equivalent, *oikonomos*, the administration in the world of "the enterprise of God which he initiated in Jesus Christ." Missionary, he says, refers to authority rather than to function—the bearing of a message which is given by God—thus the missionary is a steward and the steward a missionary. Frederick Herzog examines the twin concepts within the context of the faith, viewing them in their Biblical setting, their Biblical background, and their present-day relevance. The two cannot be spoken of separately, he affirms, for "mission begins when a steward seeks to awaken stewardship in his neighbor and realizes that there is no limit to his responsibility for neighbor."

While each of the writers refers to specific Biblical teachings, none presumes to set forth a systematic study of passages from Scripture which treat stewardship and mission. We therefore would commend for study the Bible expositions included in the report on a Consultation held in Switzerland in 1961. Prof. Eduard Schweizer classifies passages under headings of "household," "house-building," and "stewardship," all of which belong to the same etomological family in the original.[4] Rev. Hans-Rudei Weber in his study of the laity shows the similarity between stewardship emphasis and the "priestly sacrifice in which

[3] *Ibid.*, p. 38.
[4] *Ibid.*, pp. 1-14.

God's people offers itself in love and obedience to God and in love and sacrifice for men." [5] Stewards of the new life, Dr. Weber insists, are believers in renewal, in the glorious renewal to come, and in the present growth of newness.[6] Rev. Herbert Reich discusses the gifts (*charisma*) as the service of the steward in fulfilling the service expected of him, and of the New Testament meanings of stewardship (*diakonia*) which go beyond "living service." [7] Dr. Schweizer in his exposition of Romans 12:1-8 points up the particularity of God's grace as always taking a specific form, and the need for translating stewardship into our particular situation.

[5] *Ibid.*, pp. 15-17.
[6] *Ibid.*, pp. 18-20.
[7] *Ibid.*, pp. 21-23.

1

THE THEOLOGY
OF STEWARDSHIP

Elmer J. F. Arndt

Stewardship is one of the most familiar words in the vocabulary of American Christians. Yet is would be a grave misunderstanding if we began with the assumption that we already know, and *know* as a matter of course, what stewardship is. It would be equally mistaken to think that such a theme as "the theology of stewardship" required of us only that there be developed an acceptable rationalization of what we are already doing or wanted others to do.

If the theology of stewardship is a serious undertaking and if it intended to be something more than an attractively "packaged" appeal for financial support of a worthy social institution, then it is urgent that we come to our inquiry with an openness to instruction, a receptive spirit, and a willingness to be guided into what may turn out to be surprising and unexpected new directions and dimensions. Here also we must come prepared to receive the kingdom "like a little child." For the question with which a serious theological inquiry concerning stewardship has to grapple is not How can man's religiosity be most successfully exploited to support our programs? but, rather, What does God have to teach us through the Scriptures, illuminated by the Spirit, concerning our relation to Him and specifically that relation viewed from the angle of vision we call stewardship?

1

To essay a "theology of stewardship" is—as in any theology —first of all to invoke the Spirit and to listen to the Scriptures, and only then to proceed to a statement of teaching—and the statement of teaching only as a response to God's revealing of Himself, thus always subject to his correction.

THE TEST PATTERN OF STEWARDSHIP

There are three grand motifs which the theology of steward-ship emphatically sounds: (1) stewardship is our thankful wit-ness to God's benevolence; (2) stewardship is our obedient wit-ness to God's sovereignty; and (3) stewardship is our faithful response to God's call to serve our fellow men in the service of Christ.

In each of these motifs stewardship is a vital, personal re-sponse to God's acting towards us. Taken together, the three motifs make it very clear that stewardship is integral to the life of faith—indeed, it is but another name for that response of faith which God's immeasurable gift in Christ awakens in us. Stewardship is a central, not a peripheral, concern of the Chris-tian. It is not a matter of a nicely calculated greater or lesser contribution, but a total response of a total person to God's act of unreserved self-giving.

THANKFULNESS

Our first motif is that stewardship is our thankful witness to God's benevolence. The rightful order is the prior giving of God and our stewardship as responsive to His giving. The pre-venience of God's gracious giving culminating in self-donation in Christ is the foundation and source of stewardship.

The divine benevolence is certainly not a new theme to mem-bers of the Christian church. That benevolence is fundamental to prayer, as it is to stewardship. Just as the ground of our confi-dence in prayer is God's willingness to give us what we need before we ask, so also the spring of our stewardship is the abundance of God's giving to us. These gifts are not apportioned according to our deserts. Rather they are His free gifts to the undeserving, gifts to which no man can make a valid claim.

Because we know God's benevolence to be free and undeserved, the living spring of our practice of stewardship is gratitude. Stewardship is eucharistic. And as the early eucharistic prayers of the church expressed thankfulness for the whole range of God's goodness, so the steward of God rejoices to keep before him the fullness of God's benevolence.

God gives life—our existence and our being as creatures made in His image. He gives us personal being, life in community, and communion with himself. He has set our lives in the world of nature—the great primary environment—which at once supports and challenges us.

He maintains in the world of nature an orderliness which is the presupposition of all our scientific inquiry. He does not abandon us because we are disordered and make disorder in the world of history. He remains faithful to us even when we are unfaithful to Him. Both His judgments and His mercy are evidence of his faithfulness.

His holy love prompts the gift of his Son. In Jesus Christ He comes to us to share our common lot and to reconcile us to Himself. He comes to us in self-sacrificial love, taking on Himself the burden of our enmity and guilt, and removing for us the obstacles to communion with Himself. He delivers us from the spiritual slavery into which we have sold ourselves and grants us the gift of freedom.

God in Christ not only redeems, but also renews us, imparting His Spirit, the Lord the Life-giver and the Bond of love. Thus He gives the supreme gift of His presence with us and among us together with the gifts the Spirit bestows. And that gift of the Spirit is itself the guarantee of the still further gift of the consummation of the rule of God and the fulfillment of His gracious purpose. God gives the power to live the new life in Christ now and the hope which together constitute the renewal of man in life eternal. He constitutes His church, the people of God, the body of Christ, and the sphere in which the Holy Spirit works to bind men to Christ and to each other in a genuine community.

God's gifts of creation, redemption, and renewal elicit the response of faith which expresses itself in stewardship. For faith is the response of the whole man in trustful acceptance of God's gift and commitment to His service. Stewardship is the grateful expression in practice of the commitment included in faith. The response is without limit because the gift to which it responds is beyond any measurement. God gives Himself, and God does not want merely something from us, but nothing less than ourselves. The very self, created and recreated, which He Himself has given us, He wishes from us as our free gift to Himself.

OBEDIENCE

Stewardship is the practical expression of gratitude to the Giver of every good and perfect gift; it is also our obedient witness to God's sovereignty. It is the witness in action that we believe in God, the Creator, Redeemer, Sanctifier; that our belief in God means that we acknowledge Him as the Sovereign of our lives as well as of all things, and therefore acknowledge Him as the ultimate authority above every other authority which makes a claim on our loyalty. Stewardship is the practical expression of our assent to the divine affirmation: "I am the Lord thy God." It is our practical obedience in our administration of everything under our control—everything entrusted to us. It is the consecration of oneself and possessions to his service in the service of men.

Stewardship is the consecration of everything which is entrusted to us just because God's sovereignty embraces all things. The range of God's sovereignty is all-inclusive: the realm of nature, the sphere of cultural authorities, the principle of recompense (which is the principle of law and the law in Pauline usage), the fact of evil, and the fact of death. Creation and providence, redemption through the cross of Christ, the triumph over death in the resurrection of Christ, and the renewal of man through the Holy Spirit all manifest God's sovereignty and His sovereignty as a sovereignty of grace rather than a sovereignty of sheer power.

The correlate to God's sovereignty is our stewardship, for our stewardship is the acknowledgment in practice that we do not have the absolute right of disposal of ourselves and our property. In short, we are stewards and not owners. Stewardship is the affirmation in practical living that we are not our own, but belong to Christ, the Lord, who gave Himself for us.

Likewise, stewardship is the expression of our obedience in mission. We are accountable for our administration of the mysteries of God. For a Christian church, local or otherwise, to act as though it could determine to whom it ministers and who can be included or excluded from its fellowship by any standards other than those intrinsic to the gospel is to deny its stewardship. To make such criteria as class or race conditions of membership in the local church or the larger fellowship is tantamount to substituting man's authority for God's, and falsely asserting our possession of the mysteries of God.

Stewardship is witness that we confess in fact and in act the Lordship of Jesus Christ. It is the active testimony that we are given all things, including ourselves, so that ourselves first of all and all things can be given for the other. Stewardship is witness; it is the martyrdom which is the privilege of every Christian. It is the witness to the gift already received, and it is the witness to the living hope that God will fulfill his promises to establish his kingdom.

RESPONSIVENESS

Finally, stewardship is our faithful response to God's call to serve our fellow men in the service of Christ. He has commissioned and elected us by our baptism into Christ and His church to continue the ministry of Christ, from whose ministry all our ministries are derived. The practice of stewardship is our participation in Christ's continuing ministry to His people and mankind. It is the expression of our incorporation into the body of Christ.

The whole church (every member of it) is called to share in Christ's continuing ministry. Those who are conventionally called lay people are in a special sense the church in the world, and the ordained members are in a special sense the church ministering to its members.

The mission to which the whole church is called is a witness to God's great act of reconciliation in the cross of Jesus Christ, to God's righteousness, peace, and justice, to the living Lord Jesus Christ, crucified for our sins and raised from the dead for our renewal.

The church witnesses to the lordship of Christ; its mission is to confront men with His claim to be the Lord of all and the Lord of the whole of men's lives. Stewardship is the demonstration in practice that Christ is Lord—personally and corporately.

Because stewardship is the practice of Christ's lordship, it is consequently our service to men. It is faith and hope and love in action. It is offering to men the best we have to offer—the gift we ourselves have received. Since we live by and from God's gift, we have received the freedom to participate without anxious reservation in the struggle for justice for our fellow man and peace in the world and in the various forms of voluntary service for the well-being of our fellow men.

Stewardship is nothing less—and there cannot be anything greater—than self-sacrificial giving. It is a style of life which holds for the Christian and for the institutions the Christian community develops as vehicles of its life and mission. If the common life of the body of Christ provides the opportunity for each member to make the contribution he has been enabled to make through his particular endowment, the institutions of the common life present an ever-present challenge for efficient administration and useful service of men. Christian institutions—the institutional church and the whole array of "church-related" institutions—are perennially a "problem" for serious Christian stewardship. For institutions are power structures, and the tendency of power structures (and those who control them) is to maintain themselves rather than to lose themselves in the service of others.

DISTORTED VIEWS OF STEWARDSHIP

In concluding this sketch of the theology of stewardship, two common perversions of stewardship should be noticed.

The first perversion is the notion that stewardship has to do only with money. The use of money is indeed included in our stewardship. However, stewardship has to do first of all with the *self*. The first word in the lexicon of stewardship is that God claims us in our total being for Himself and His service. To restrict our stewardship to the use of money is not a limitation of our stewardship, but a perversion of it. An even greater perversion of stewardship, consequently, is to restrict our stewardship to a percentage—whether small or large—of our money incomes.

The second perversion of stewardship is to limit it to the support of our local church or our denomination, for this limitation is practical denial of the mission entrusted to us and of our status as stewards rather than owners. The local church, the conference, the denomination are all too limited for a witness to our faith, hope, and love responding to God who reconciled the world to Himself.

The norm by which our stewardship is tested is that of the Steward, Jesus Christ, who gave Himself to the uttermost. And that stewardship has a word to say to the institutions we cherish as well as to our personal living and acting.

Stewardship is orientated and directed to the other; it is, indeed directed to two others, each distinct yet inseparable. When directed toward God, stewardship is doxological and eucharistic. When directed toward the church, our fellow believers, and our world of neighbors, it is love in action.

Stewardship is included in the love which is faith in action. Like faith, of which it is a practical expression, it has its spring and source in the benevolence of God.

2

THE CONTINUING INCARNATION

Roy Pearson

Before taking the full plunge into the theology of stewardship and mission, let us dangle our feet for a moment in a few miscellaneous assumptions along the shore. With each of the three nouns (theology, stewardship, and mission) let us assume the adjective "Christian." As a working definition of theology, we might accept "the science which treats of the existence, character, and attributes of God, and of His laws and government." For our present purpose let us disregard Webster's definition of a steward as "a household officer on a lord's estate having charge of the cattle," and interpret stewardship to mean the essential status of man in his wholeness, considered not as an owner, but as an owner's agent. Missions can be regarded as stewardship in action, and the theology of stewardship and missions can be assumed to be the study of God's relationship to his property.

If relevant theology is incredibly more complex than we have sometimes thought, it is nonetheless incredibly more simple. It is certainly more complex. The rigid fundamentalist, for instance, is clearly mistaken when he supposes that the narrow borders of his mind encompass the vast expanses of God's being. There is more to God than he knows, and, speaking with assurance, he is assuredly unjustified in much of his speaking. No man has seen God at any time; no man comprehends the fullness of His will; and whenever we say, "God is . . ." or "God wants . . ." or "God does . . . ," we make an affirmation which has no warrant without the explicit or implicit preface, "I think that . . ."

Yet relevant theology is also more simple than some would have us believe. God did not send His Son into the world to bewilder His creatures, but to save them. He is not playing games with His people. He does not give us enough knowledge to satisfy our curiosity, but He does give enough to meet the needs of life. It has been said that God must have loved the common people because He made so many of them, and it is inconceivable that any theology which is essential for human life is a theology which cannot be understood without a college education. The significant elements of theology are simple elements, susceptible to clear statement and understandable by people of average intelligence. When theology becomes complex the reason is not that the subject defies clear formulation, but rather that the interpreters are confused.

GOD AND GOD ALONE

Inescapably, the theology of stewardship and missions begins with God, and we may as well admit at once that the terminology of the theological task is utterly inadequate. It is a broken staff, a leaky trumpet, and a flickering candle. Vocabulary of human origin embodies the only words the world possesses. Although theology concerns the world, its origins are other-worldly. Thus, when we speak about God, our tongues are tied—tied loosely enough to permit us to speak with the coveted clarity.

Nevertheless, we still must speak. And the indispensable foundation of a Christian theology of stewardship and missions is deity which actually exists—almighty, eternal, unique, and personal. He is almighty: whatever can be done He can do. He is eternal: there was no beginning to His almightiness, and there will be no end. He is unique: there is neither duplicate nor rival of Him.

Most important of all, God is an actually existing, personal Being. Stewardship and missions involve relationship, and the involved relationship is not between living men and lifeless concepts. In one sense, God is not a person because He is not *limited* by personal attributes. In another sense, He is a person because whatever else He may be, the wholeness of Him *includes* personal attributes. When Jesus spoke of God as "Father," He was not dealing in philosophical abstractions. Jesus was stating a relationship in terms of personal commitment. Although "Father" is certainly inadequate as an all-inclusive description of God, it is certainly more accurate than any description which equates God with His creation or with the other images by which we attempt to transcend the imperfections of language.

In the words of John Baillie, "A pagan is not a man who does not believe in and worship deity, but a man who believes in and worships too many deities. He is not a man who has no religion but a man who . . . has too much." [1] From one point of view, the Christian understanding of stewardship and missions depends not on additions to deity, but on substractions from it. For Spinoza, God minus the world equaled nothing, but for the Christian, God minus the world equals God.[2] God is not many: God is one—one not only in the sense that there is not a separately existing God for each of the world's great religions, but one also in the sense that, in all that is, He is the one being to whom the word "God" can rightly be applied. God is not what we wish He might be: He is what He is. He moves in His creation, but He is separable from it. Past man's definition, He is yet theoretically definable. Beyond description by His creatures, He can describe Himself. God is not everything. If there are affirmations to be made about Him, there are also negations. There are things which God is not.

Among the things that God is must be included an actually existing being—almighty, eternal, unique, and personal. He is being capable of meaningful relationship with His human creatures. We cannot know Him completely, but we can know Him.

[1] John Baillie, *The Sense of the Presence of God* (New York: Charles Scribner's Sons, 1962), p. 170.
[2] William Ralph Inge, *Vale* (London: Longmans, Green and Company, 1934), pp. 105, 106.

And more importantly, He knows us. He is alive, and He is conscious. He is aware, and He can respond.

ONE GREAT BIG UNIVERSE

From God Himself the theology of stewardship and missions moves, in the second place, to *God and the universe*, and in this connection the essential affirmations are that God creates and owns, and that what God creates and owns is the universe.

Take the second affirmation first: what we are talking about here is not simply the part, the earth, but rather the whole, the universe. Early in history man thought that the earth had many gods and every tribe had its own. As civilization progressed wise men understood that God was not many but one, and that whatever existed on earth or beyond, was under the one God's dominion. "In the beginning God created the heavens and the earth" (Genesis 1:1). That is to say, God created everything. Surely we shall not be forced to take again the painful steps of that theological evolution which centuries ago claimed space for God no less than earth. There is not one god for the earth, another for Mars, and still another for Venus. There is simply and only God, the one Lord of the earth as well as the space and substance beyond earth.

Our first affirmation is: God's relationship to the universe is that He creates and owns it. The word "creates" is used rather than "created" because the God whose original creation is attested by Scripture daily reveals His continuing creation in a universe constantly renewed. I say that *God* creates because only God *can* create. Man himself does not create nor will he do so even if he makes himself life's midwife in his laboratories. It is only God who brings into being the original substance of the unverse. Man can do no more than rearrange what God has already created. It is of little consequence *how* God creates— whether by spurts or steadily, whether by repeated fiat or unbroken evolution. The important affirmation is that for the origin of the universe God alone is ultimately responsible.

Moreover, God owns it. "The earth is the Lord's," the psalmist said (Psalm 24:1). Nor should it be necessary to point out that what is true of the earth is also true of the universe. God created everything, and what He created He possesses. God permits the use of His creation but does not surrender the title. We buy a piece of land and think we own it, but we deceive ourselves. We compete with Russia in the moon race and assume that the moon will belong to the nation that reaches it first, but we are wrong. The universe is not man's property, neither by right of seizure nor by right of purchase.

The universe is God's property, in part, because He created it. It is God's property in another sense because whatever immortality man may possess or be granted, God retains control of His creation. Man can do no more than adapt small portions of it temporarily for his own uses. From man's point of view he can improve or destroy property. But, in the physical universe, man is a swiftly transient being. No man in history existed prior to God and the physical universe. When a man's life is ended there will still be God and the universe. At the moment of death man is separated from his possessions. That segment of the universe which he thought that he owned is inexorably taken from his hands by Him who really owns it. In his relation to the universe immortal man is desperately mortal, and his mortality makes a pretense of his claim to be an owner. Ownership involves the right to speak the final word about the property possessed, and the right to speak the final word about the universe is not the prerogative of man, but of God. God created everything that is, and He owns it. The universe is the Lord's.

TENANCY AND LIFE TENURE

The third step forward is to turn from God and the universe to *the universe and man*, and we have already anticipated the principal assertions.

Everybody knows that something new appeared on the earth with the coming of man. Whatever the continuities between his immediate evolutionary predecessors and man himself, it is hard to escape the conviction of a jarring discontinuity. "Man is a conglomeration of transformed groceries," one writer claims,[3] and, looking at him with one eye, who can deny that? "Man is like the apes," the scientist declares, and, looking at him with the same eye, who can deny that? But the second eye adds a deeper perspective, and long before Christ the distinctions of man were apparent. Man was created for dominion. He was made but little lower than the angels, and he was crowned with glory and honor. Man is a conglomeration of transformed groceries, but how much more! Man is like the apes, but how different!

Yet at this point in the development of a theology of stewardship and missions the significant assertions are those already suggested in connection with God and the universe. Man is a creature. Man is a dependent. Man is a tenant.

The places of men on the earth are like those of summer residents in one of the small post offices on Cape Cod. You arrive in the town about the first of July, and you give the postmaster fifty cents. That entitles you to use one of the boxes for the summer months. You get a receipt for your money and the combination to the box, and the postmaster puts a little tag on the inner side of the box with your name on it. This is *your* box: it is set aside for your use, and you have the exclusive rights to it. But on Labor Day you go back to the city, and your box is *yours* no longer. Your name tag is removed, and when another summer rolls around somebody else gets the summer-long exclusive.

When man appeared on the earthly scene there was something about him which he did not share with any other earthly creature; but he was nonetheless a creature, a dependent, a tenant. A self-made man is a contradiction in terms. Man is incapable of making himself. It is God who has made us, and not we ourselves. We are fully dependent on God for our being and we are but tenants in God's furnished apartments on earth. We possess nothing. We borrow or steal, and we use; but we do not own. There is no owner but God.

[3] Theodosius Dobzhansky, "Man Consorting with Things Eternal," Harlow Shapley (ed.) *Science Ponders Religion* (New York: Appleton-Century-Crofts, 1960), p. 117.

Furthermore—and we have also partially anticipated this assertion—there is no reason to believe that earthly man is the only child of the heavenly Father and that other planets must be empty of comparable beings. It took men a long time to get over the idea that God had no other children than their tribe, nation, race, or religion. It is not too early for men to rid themselves of the idea that God could have no other children than earthly man or even simply man. Perhaps He does not have other children, but perhaps He does. Perhaps we have human brothers on other planets, and on other planets perhaps we have brothers who are not "human" at all. In categories above the animal and in areas beyond the earth, the time may yet come for the lion to lie down with the lamb. We are not necessarily being presumptuous to assume that the exploration of space will inevitably prove man to be the lion.

Man, then, is a creature, a dependent, and a tenant. He may be alone with his God in a universe which God creates, but then there is the outside chance he may not.

BOUNDLESS LOVE INDEED

The fourth advance toward a theology of stewardship and missions occurs when we pass from the universe and man to *man and Christ*. Something new appeared on the earth with man, but in Christ the new was even newer. There were discontinuities between man's immediate predecessors and man himself, but there are even greater discontinuities between *Before Christ* and *Anno Domini*.

Oversimplify the matter a little, and you can that B.C. man knew the what, but A.D. man knew the why. To B.C. man God was a theory, but A.D. man knew God as a fact; B.C. man saw God as an abstraction, A.D. saw God as a person. God was transcendent to B.C. man, but immanent to A.D. man. The B.C. God was one of justice who in A.D. was clearly recognized as a God of love. We recognize, of course, the inadequacies of such contrasts, but the main thrust is still valid. That God so loved the world that He gave it His Son says a great deal about why God created the world in the first place and what position man holds in His continuing attention. That God's Son was Jesus says a great deal about what God is like and what God intends.

The implications of these revelations are many. At the risk of being repetitious, I had better stress that one of them is not that God's love for the earth excludes the possibility of His love for other worlds. In fact, the opposite is true. In one of his more conservative opinions Harlow Shapley estimates that there are at least "ten billion planets suitable for organic life something like that on the earth," [4] and the assumption that in all of His creation God loved only the earth is hardly reasonable. Rather, we need only insist that God's love for other worlds need not diminish His love for the earth. Does not a parent love *all* of his children, and does the fact that he loves John reduce his love for Mary? If God sent His Son to the earth, could He not also send Him, say, to Mars, and would His mission to Mars lessen His meaning for the earth?

In terms of the earth itself, one aspect of Christ's meaning for man which cannot be escaped in a theology of stewardship and missions is its sheer materialism.

Whatever else men could say after Christ, they could not say rightly that the interests of holiness were only with spirit. In one sense Christianity might be "out of this world," but in another sense it was squarely in the middle of the world. God had become incarnate. He had made Himself flesh.

Another aspect of Christ's meaning for man is its universality. God's concern is not only for Americans, not simply for white men, not just for Christians. His concern is for the *world*, and He sent His Son for the *world* for *all* men, *all* women, *all* children.

And still another aspect is the supremacy of love over power. The hand that rules, Christ showed, is moved by the heart that cares. Thenceforth, men had evidence that God's creation was not an act of self-aggrandizement, that He loved His human creatures enough to suffer death for their redemption, and that His love had so mastered His power that what He loved, if it died with Him, would rise with Him, and with Him live for evermore.

[4] Harlow Shapley, "Stars, Ethics and Survival," *op. cit.*, p. 8.

Like all human beings and institutions, the church owns nothing—not God, not Christ, not the gospel, not material goods, and not even itself. Like all human beings and institutions, the church is a creature of God, a dependent on God, and a tenant of God. But here the likeness ceases. Insofar as Christ has reproduced Himself in His Christians the stature of the church is transformed from that of a mere creaturely dependent and tenant, who occupies or otherwise employs property belonging to another, into that of a representative, an agent, a steward. Insofar as the church is the continuing incarnation, the church is the body God uses as the instrument of a love which embraces mankind and fashions the earth for its welfare. The church is the chosen people, but the life for which the church is chosen is the life of a servant. The truth is not that the church *is* a master, but that the church *has* a Master. The church is free, but the freedom of the church exists only in bondage to the church's Lord. The church is accountable. It is accountable to God, and its accountability to God is not simply to preserve God's property from destruction, but to use God's property for God's purposes.

There is so much that could be said on this subject that one is tempted to end the matter with what has been said, but let me put a little flesh on the bones through two experiences on a recent trip to Europe under the auspices of the American Association of Theological Schools. The first occurred as we drove through Holland, Belgium, France, Germany, Italy, then Austria and Switzerland. Again and again we talked with people who had traveled more widely than ourselves, and again and again we heard the comment of American servicemen that, given their choice, they would retire in Portugal. The scenery was beautiful, houses were cheap, prices were low, servants were available, life was pleasant. But, one night we talked with a man from Kenya who was actually looking for a retirement home. He told us that Portugal was the one place in which he could never retire. There were too many poor people, and he could not stand his own prosperity in such proximity to so much want.

The second experience occurred on a Sunday morning in the

military chapel at the Alpine Inn in Berchtesgaden, Germany. Behind me was a father who, at the opening of the service, had given his little son a coin for the offering. But when the plate was passed, the results of the boy's meditation became apparent. "I'm not putting this in!" I heard him whisper to his father. "Oh yes, you are!" said his father. "No, I'm not!" the boy insisted. "I'm not! I'm not!"

It seems to me that these two experiences have considerable relevance to a theology of stewardship and missions. For a church whose self-image is that of a steward there is clear theological warrant that it go to "Portugal," not to retire, but rather so to force itself to look at the poor in body and spirit that it actually see and understand them. For a church whose self-image is that of a steward there is clear theological warrant that it recognize its riches as the gift of its Father, that it comprehend the Father's purpose in the giving, and that it consider no Christians well-dressed without holes in their pockets. And I wonder about the implications of Christian theology for churches enjoying wealth in the midst of poverty, churches growing fat in the midst of starvation, churches standing safe in the midst of danger, churches claiming privilege in the midst of persecution, and churches hoarding light in the midst of darkness. In the sixteenth century it was told of Linacre that late in life he, a priest who had received much ecclesiastical preferment, read the Sermon on the Mount for the first time. He was utterly amazed. "Either this is not the Gospel," he exclaimed, "or we are not Christians," and, refusing to contemplate the possibility of the latter alternative, he flung the book from him and went back to his medical studies.[10] And I wonder if one of the surest implications of Christian theology is not that many Christian churches are not "Christian" at all.

MAKING MEN WHOLE

In the seventh and penultimate step we pass from the church and stewardship to *stewardship and missions*, and I consider

[10] See R. W. Chambers, *Thomas More* (London: Jonathan Cape, Ltd., 1953), p. 84.

missions to be simply the joyful implementation of stewardship. We are told that we may tell. We are empowered that we may share. We are blessed that we may become an instrument of blessing. And the telling, sharing, and blessing are acts, not of burdensome duty, but of grateful privilege. Missions is stewardship in action, and the action of missions is the action of bearers of glad tidings.

In the twentieth century of the church's existence it is probably unnecessary to remind ourselves that missions is not an adjunct of the church, not one function among many. Missions is the whole purpose of the church. It is the church doing what the church ought to be doing. Furthermore, we scarcely require the admonition that if missions is the whole purpose of the church, it is also the whole purpose of the *whole* church. Missions is no longer crudely geographical in the sense that one nation is always the sender and another always the receiver. Wherever the church is, the church is a mission. But neither is missions any longer crudely hierarchical in the sense that ministers are meant for missions, and laymen are meant only for money. The *whole* church is a mission, and the church's mission is often better furthered in an office, a schoolroom, or a kitchen than in a pulpit. And further still, we hardly need to belabor the fact that if missions is the whole purpose of the whole church, it is also the whole purpose of the whole church for the whole universe. The field is the world in the sense that no aspect of man's life on the earth is irrelevant to the church's mission, but it is also the world in the sense that the church's mission is relevant to any world beyond the earth.

Let me emphasize instead that any significant theology of the church's mission reveals it to be initially divisive, ultimately unifying, and always desperately urgent. It is *initially* divisive because it is inescapably exclusive. "A half-way house to the bold affirmation that all religions are equally false," said the Lindsay Commission, "is the assertion that all religions are equally true." [11] But Christian theology claims that Christ is distinc-

[11] Hugh Vernon White, A *Theology for Christian Missions* (Chicago: Willett, Clark and Company, 1937), p. 105.

tively the truth, and unavoidably it sets the Christian gospel in opposition to other gospels.

Ultimately, however, the mission of the church is a unifying mission for the reasons set forth by John Baillie:

> . . . if it had been so that each could find God in his own way, each would be finding him without at the same time finding his brother . . . Was it not then a gracious ordering of things on God's part that there should be ultimate salvation for us all in only one Name; that we can meet with him only by meeting with one another; by betaking ourselves all together to one place—to one "green hill far away"; by encountering there a single Figure to whom we offer our united allegiance; by listening to the self-same story; by reading in the same sacred book; by being baptized into the same fellowship; by eating and drinking at the same Holy Table; so that "there is no difference between Jew and Greek for the same Lord is Lord of all," and "here there is not Greek and Jew, circumcised and uncircumcised, barbarian, Scythian, slave or free man, but Christ is all and in all"? Is it not true that we cannot have real unity until we all have "the same Lord"? [12]

And *always* the mission of the church is desperately urgent because the choice is no longer between living together and living apart, but between living together and not living. It is desperately urgent because God, who owns what He creates, is being robbed of His creation. It is desperately urgent because God's children cannot love their Father fully without also loving their brothers.

THIS SPIRIT-FILLED MOMENT

And now the final step: *missions and the Holy Spirit*. To use the somewhat awkward but none the less meaningful terminology of two contemporary theologians, I take the Holy Spirit to represent in this instance, on the one hand, "the *isness* of the *was*" and, on the other hand, "the *isness* of the *shall be*." [13]

---

[12] Baillie, *op. cit.*, pp. 208, 209.
[13] See Claude H. Thompson, *Theology of the Kerygma* (Englewood Cliffs, N.J.: Prentice-Hall, Inc., 1962), p. 23.

In other words, for an adequate theology of stewardship and missions we need something more than the *wasness* either of God's original creation or of His revelation in the earthly life of Jesus and something more even than the *shall be* of God's ultimate triumph foreshadowed in Christ's resurrection; and in the Holy Spirit the *was* and the *shall be* become the needed *is*.

In the subways of Boston signs are posted that announce: THIRD RAIL ALIVE. There is something suggestive about that warning as we try to fashion a Christian theology of stewardship and missions. We believe in God, the Father almighty, Maker of heaven and earth. That is the first rail. We also believe in Jesus Christ, His Son, who was born, killed, and raised again from the dead. That is the second rail. But it is the third rail which is immediately and dangerously alive—the Holy Spirit, moving in the world today, touching the heart of every creature, judging, persuading, pleading, prodding; and in the Holy Spirit lies the final hope of the church in its stewardship and mission.

It is all very well to insist that God never changes; all very well to affirm that Jesus is the same yesterday, today, and forever; all very well to point out that human nature does not seem very different in the twentieth century after Christ than it was in the tenth century before Him. But the environment of the gospel is constantly being altered. Change and decay we see all around us, and all around us we see change and new growth. To that environment the mission of the church is the same today as it was in the first century, but to imitate the methods of the first-century church may not be to imitate the first-century church. For it was the genius of the best parts of the first-century church that they matched their methods, not only with their message, but also with their goals. If nothing else, the noblest portions of the early church were amazingly pragmatic. In their own particular place and time they did precisely what needed to be done to accomplish what they knew that they were called to do.

The early church attributed both the wisdom and the power of its strategy to the God who, to be sure, had created the world and who, to be sure, had revealed Himself to men in Jesus Christ, but who—wonder beyond all other wonders—

3

TO HAVE AND TO HAVE NOT

Ralph Douglas Hyslop

Many years ago a Man stood up in a synagogue in Nazareth and read the words of the prophet Isaiah:

> The Spirit of the Lord is upon me,
>> because he has anointed me to preach good news to the poor (61:1-2).
>
> He has sent me to proclaim release to the captives
>> and recovering of sight to the blind,
>> to set at liberty those who are oppressed,
>> to proclaim the acceptable year of the Lord (Luke 4:18-19).

When He had finished reading, He said, "Today this scripture has been fulfilled in your hearing."

The Man who read the lines from the Prophet Isaiah and spoke that dramatic sentence in commentary upon them, a few minutes later was almost lynched by the citizens of His home town. His followers, in the earliest days of Christianity and through the centuries of its history, have often fared no better. A full century after the Emancipation Proclamation Negro students have suffered cruel insults and physical violence while peacefully asserting their full civil rights, guaranteed by law. The officers of the law, in these situations, have often acted with discipline and restraint while placing, *not* the attackers,

25

but the attacked in jail. And many of them, as the police vans carried them off, were heard singing the songs which utter with profound faith God's promise proclaimed by Isaiah over 2500 years ago: "to set at liberty those who are oppressed."

There is one striking resemblance and one equally arresting contrast between the people who heard Jesus in the synagogue at Nazareth and those who hear today the same promise affirmed by Negro students. In both cases the people who hear and react with anger and violence know their sacred Scriptures: the Jews knew the Law and the Prophets, and the heavily Protestant South knows the Holy Bible. But in Nazareth that day the hearers in the synagogue were incensed because Jesus was saying to them that He could not do His work of healing and release in His own home town for "no prophet is acceptable in his own country." Today the reverse is true. The people who see Negro students sitting at lunch counters and hear them singing the songs of promise are afraid that the things proclaimed by Isaiah, fulfilled by Jesus, *will* happen right there in their own home towns. And this is intolerable!

Now, of course, given our choice we will identify ourselves with the synagogue congregation in Nazareth rather than with our fellow countrymen in Alabama, Georgia, and Mississippi. At least the former *wanted* the prophecy of Isaiah to be fulfilled, even if they could not understand why it is so difficult for the prophet to be accepted "in his own country."

CONSCIENCE IN TURMOIL

The first hard word that must be spoken is that we are not given that choice. We no longer have Jesus with us in the flesh. We have only the troublesome reminder, provided by his present-day followers, that He still today says to us, "*Today* this scripture has been fulfilled in your hearing." He is not of our country. We do not live in Nazareth. There is no profit in speculating about what we might have done had we been in the synagogue that day. We know what we *do* when, in the persons of His ardent disciples, He confronts us with the fulfillment of the ancient prophecy right where we are. If we are honest, de-spite the greater suavity of our language, we *are* represented in the man who yells at the sit-down demonstrator, "Get the hell out of here." We *are* represented in the sweet Southern girl of "Ole Miss," home of the "Miss Americas," who cries to James Meredith, "Somebody ought to kill you."

If this appears to be a rather discouraging introduction to a discussion of a "theology of stewardship and mission," it is not because I am just another of these gloomy theologians who can see nothing but evil in man. I am, as it happens, a rather op-timistic type. I happen to think that at Nazareth I would have been far back in the crowd, out of sight of the cliff and pushing only to get a better view. And I am quite sure that were I in Oxford, Mississippi, or Birmingham, Alabama, today I would be doing just what I am doing at Broadway and 120th Street in New York City: carrying on with my very important job and keeping out of such messy things as the active struggle for jus-tice (not tolerance or good will—I believe in these and express it) in race relations. It's strange that Birmingham should be involved, for another minister whose theology is probably faulty and whose poetry would never deserve the Nobel Prize, wrote some lines about his nation's Birmingham and a visitor there:

> When Jesus came to Birmingham,
> > they simply passed Him by,
> They never hurt a hair of Him,
> > they only let Him die;
> For men have grown more tender,
> > and they would not give Him pain,
> They only just passed down the street,
> > and left Him in the rain.

You can see what bad poetry that is. Nevertheless, it seems a bit more truly descriptive of my attitude than the film we can all see about our own Birmingham, done some time ago for tele-vision by Howard K. Smith. Men were being beaten up in Birmingham, and I felt very indignant, and also a little com-forted, for I would never do that. I lost the feeling of comfort a short time later when I reflected that I would certainly never *suffer* that either, in deliberate, courageous, and continuing pursuit of justice for all.

The reason for this apparently non-theological introduction is simply that Christian theology is theology of the Word of God. And every part of the New Testament reminds us that this Word of God is a living Word, clothed in flesh and named Jesus whom we call Lord and Savior. The written word in the New Testament depends upon him. Every word of theology must have its reference to this living Word and the witness the Scriptures bear to Him. So the introduction is hardly non-theological, and it is not even introduction. It is our theme itself.

CONFRONTING THE PAINFUL TRUTH

For I am convinced, as a theologian, that there is something "phony" about any theology which does not hurt, causing pain first to him who writes it and then to those who hear it or read it. I am not referring to the pain caused by strange words, long sentences, and unfamiliar ideas; these are incidental and often quite unnecessary in the first place. I am speaking of the pain that has some relationship to penitence, the hurt that is born in the realization that we don't really want Him around—this one whom we call Lord. It is hard to bear—this sudden awareness that a great many of our words and even a large proportion of our deeds are unrecognized attempts to escape Him. Let's begin honestly by facing this very painful fact, for there is no Christian understanding of stewardship and mission which is not grounded in the knowledge that the Lord whom we *say* we serve is the same Lord whom we seek, ever so cleverly, to escape. I shall not attempt to catalogue the ways in which we manage this escape from Jesus the living Lord. You have your ways; I have mine.

Let me, then, record the painful conviction that the treasure of which we are stewards, the truth which impels us to mission is *never* ours. We cannot possess it, though the New Testament holds out the great hope that we may more and more be possessed by it. The very words we use are faulty, for this treasure, this truth is not "it" but "He," Jesus of Nazareth, Savior of the world. When Paul in his letters goes through the linguistic acrobatics that seem at times to be "double-talk," he is trying to put into words what is almost incommunicable and yet is the very heart of all Christian experiences. We have died with Christ and been raised with Him to newness of life—yet the old nature still lives in us. We have the mind of Christ and yet are capable of the most blatant betrayal of His commands to us. It is strange that a great writer of our day, the late Ernest Hemingway, a seeming celebrant of the glories of an heroic paganism, should have given a title to a novel which precisely sums up this truth: *To Have and Have Not.*

Many of us sing or recite weekly in our churches these words of the offertory:

> 1. We give thee but thine own,
> Whate'er the gift may be:
> All that we have is thine alone,
> A trust, O Lord, from thee.

Perhaps we stop at the first stanza. Two later stanzas amplify what is a very sound theology, though echoing, as so much of our religious literature does, the past of an agricultural rather than the present of an industrial age:

> 2. May we thy bounties thus
> As stewards true receive,
> And gladly, as thou blessest us,
> To thee our first fruits give.
>
> .   .   .   .   .
>
> 6. And we believe thy word,
> Though dim our faith may be;
> Whate'er for thine we do, O Lord,
> We do it unto thee.[1]

Ponder for a moment the word, "firstfruits." What a lovely and nostalgic image it invokes. Reinhold Niebuhr once recounted in a vivid fashion his planning of a truly Biblical har-

[1] William Walshom How, 1823-1897.

vest festival in his Detroit church. The children played a special role for they were to bring the "firstfruits": the produce of the land offered unto the Lord in grateful remembrance of His bounty in nature. The young pastor had delightful visions of the multi-colored array of the fruits of the harvest heaped about the altar on this Thanksgiving Day. He had forgotten only one thing. This was a definitely urban parish and everything the children brought was in cans. Perhaps the profound understanding of the meaning of Christian faith in a technical civilization, which we owe to Reinhold Niebuhr, began that day. For the important point is not the form and substance of what we possess, but the recognition that "all that we have is Thine alone, a trust, O Lord, from Thee."

PREFABRICATED GIVING

Now, seriously, does anyone contend that this confession is at the center or even on the periphery of our modern life as we understand it? Corporation executives, large stockholders, and even moderate-income folk are inclined to utter something like these words in different form and through clenched teeth as tax returns are labored over and checks sent to the district office of the Internal Revenue Service—if the money has not already been withheld. But this is no glad giving, despite the fact that concern for equal opportunity and human dignity is as least not wholly lost in our nation's concentration upon "defense."

And what about these terrifying weapons of defense which we possess? Our one surest point of union with our Soviet enemies is that together we can, if we choose, blow up the world and all its people—assuring even the few survivors that their children unto the ninth or ninetieth generation will bear in their genes the mark of our majestic atomic power. "All that we have is Thine alone . . ."—even these earth and life shattering weapons too? I spoke of the coexistence in our two nations of this mighty power, but in terms of *their* official faith, they at least do not have to face this terrible question. It is we have piously inserted in "The Pledge of Allegiance" the words,

"This nation *under God*"; dialectical materialists have their problems, even their ideological disputes, but they are free of this terrible burden. If God does not exist, then there can be no constraint to render Him an accounting for that which is a trust from Him.

Perhaps we can say that all these things, so terrible and wonderful, are not of God, but of Satan. I am the last one to speak lightly of the devil; I have long felt that he was entitled to a larger place in our theology. To our Puritan predecessors in the seventeenth and eighteenth centuries he seemed to be forever engaged in his nefarious plots against personal morality. I suspect that he has succeeded admirably in adapting himself to our more complex industrial civilization and may be very busily employed in his work of sabotage in a technical society. But it will not do for us to employ him to relieve us from our responsibility. This would please him greatly. It is *we* who must render an accounting to God the Creator for our use or misuse of the creative powers that He has given us. This is stewardship and it involves every possible relationship in which we are bound up with all of our fellow men.

DESIGN FOR REDEMPTIVE GIVING

No doctrine of the separation of church and state must relieve us of our high responsibility as Christian citizens to make difficult determinations concerning our actual responsibility through our government for our brother men in need in this nation and throughout the world. It is no doubt true that a very large element of self-interest enters into every action we as a nation take in foreign aid, technical assistance, even the Peace Corps, and it is also a sober truth that we shall probably continue for some time to carry the massive costs of a defense establishment which is our part of the "balance of terror" on which our present peace so precariously rests.

But let no Christian escape from this higher truth: above the nation, and even the United Nations, is the God to whom we owe full and final allegiance. He has taught us by His own self-giving that life can be lived rightly only when it is given for the more abundant life of all our fellow men. All that we have is lent to be spent for the peace and reconciliation of the nations. This, above all urgings of prudence or of fear, must be our guide as both citizens and church members. As citizens we will support to the utmost all endeavors which seek to express our concern, our caring for our brothers wherever they may dwell, whatever the color of their skin or political allegiance. Let no American who calls himself Christian dare to say that we can afford, if we must, fifty billion dollars for defense, but must cut far below 10 per cent of that total the amount we are willing to spend to help in the unceasing battle against poverty, disease, illiteracy, and tragic inequality of opportunity in other nations as well as our own. It is, I think, a very real question whether we or the world can really afford the unabated pile-up of nuclear weapons by ourselves and Russia. But we *can* and *must* afford every effort that builds world community by eliminating the myriad injustices and indignities which today degrade the human spirit.

Our nation is but formally and vaguely Christian, despite our protestations. But our churches bear no other name, no other loyalty than that of Christ. What is required of the churches in America? *It is required that they place before all of their members the call of Christ to serve in His name all the children of God to the utmost limits of our ability.* Jesus himself asks, "Why do you call me Lord, Lord, and do not the things that I bid you do?" Worship without commitment is utterly without meaning. Commitment that is cautious and prudential is without reality. The central affirmation about God in the whole of the Bible is this: *God so loved the world that He gave His only-begotten Son that all who believe in Him should not perish but have everlasting life* (John 3:16).

THE ALL-INCLUSIVE WAY

This gift, which inspires a saving trust, is simply not real for us unless it is met by the response of discipleship. We are not only to *believe* in our Lord but to *follow* Him. To be disciples means to be under discipline.

I have often wondered whether this discipleship is not too demanding, this discipline too severe. I know I cannot give myself wholly and purely as Jesus gave Himself. He is not only my elder brother, but my Savior, and it is in the realization of the immense difference between His stewardship—His mission, and my own that the truth of my deep need of His grace, His forgiving love, pours into my heart. What then can He mean when He says to His disciples, "Be ye perfect even as your Father in heaven is perfect"? (Matthew 5:48). One who knows fully the Aramaic, the language in which Jesus spoke, reports that in this language there is no word for "perfect." Jesus used an Aramaic word which can most properly be translated as not "perfect," but "all-inclusive."

Our understanding and exercise of stewardship and mission will always be human, faltering, imperfect. We are not Christ. Always we will need the aid of God's grace, which is both forgiveness and new power. But we *can* be, with all our limitations, all-inclusive. We have heard much of the ecumenical movement; I have spoken endlessly of it; some of us seem to speak of nothing else. We are called ecumaniacs. But usually, when we use the word "ecumenical" we are speaking of the essential unity of Christ's church and our responsibility to make this a manifest, visible unity. Let us think and hear and speak more of *ecumenical charity* and let us *act* in this all-inclusive way so that men everywhere may know that God loves the world, that Christ died for all men, that all are brothers and each one equally precious in the sight of his Creator and Redeemer. This is the unlimited character of our stewardship and the boundless extent of our mission. "Be ye all inclusive as your heavenly Father is."

Truman and Virginia Douglass wrote some lines for a New Year's greeting that may well serve as a sort of guideline in an understanding of stewardship and mission. Their hope for the New Year was:

> That we may know the fierce joy of living in a revolutionary time, when victims of oppression and contempt are achieving the stature of manhood and human dignity.
>
> That we may learn to measure our position in life by the

people who look at us level-eyed, not by the number upon whom we can look down.

That we may pray less for security and more for courage to do God's will.

That we may cherish as friends not those who make us comfortable but those who join us in the fight for truth and justice.

That we may trust God enough to be glad when He destroys the shoddy and corrupt things we have loved and replaces them with the clean and true things He would have us learn to love.

That we may first be willing to ask God to call us to be with Him and His purposes; then humbly ask Him to be with us and bless us.

To those who thus hope and pray, all things are possible—not because *they* are righteous or wise or powerful, but because *God* is all these things and He is God with us, Emmanuel. By him a Savior has been sent into the world and His name is Christ the Lord. This is the primary and decisive mission, for the very word mission means "sending." And we who proclaim His coming are sending Him into all the world, stewards of a great treasure not ours to hold or to abandon, but only, by His grace, to share.

4

ECONOMISTS OF THE KINGDOM

Hugh Vernon White

> This is how one should regard us, as servants of Christ and
> stewards of the mysteries of God. Moreover it is required of
> stewards that they be found trustworthy (I Corinthians
> 4:1-2).
>
> As each has received a gift, employ it for one another, as good
> stewards of God's varied grace: whoever speaks, as one who
> utters oracles of God; whoever renders service, as one who
> renders it by the strength which God supplies; in order that
> in everything God may be glorified through Jesus Christ
> (I Peter 4:10-11).

Stewardship and mission are one in the church. Both represent the orientation of the church in its work and in its preaching. Both terms indicate that the church is carrying on a work
that it did not originate, and of which it is not the proprietor,
and that it proclaims a message that it did not itself devise, but
that is entrusted to it by God. As steward, the church is a responsible general manager and administrator. Literally it is an
economist—the Greek word is *oikonómos*—administering in
the world the enterprise of God which He initiated in Jesus
Christ.

As missionary, the church proclaims to the world the gospel

of Christ. It is apostolic, and apostolic means missionary. The word signifies originally, not authority, but function. The missionary bears a message that is given to him, and he is responsible to the Lord who gave it. He goes out not to tell what he knows of himself, or to do what he wills to do, or merely to express his own goodness or good will. His supreme responsibility is to the One who sends him; he must deliver the message as he has received it, in its fullness and in its true spirit and meaning.

The steward is missionary; the missionary is steward. The church is called upon to be a good steward of God's varied grace; when it speaks—preaches or teaches—it is as "one who utters the oracles of God"; when it renders service it is "as one who renders it by the strength that God supplies."

This is the theological basis of stewardship and mission, not as a doctrine or system of beliefs, but in the primary sense of the God-controlled and God-directed life of the church. But we do need a systematic development of the theology. The greatest weakness of the church regarding the world mission, second only to our deficiency in faith and love, is the lack of a clear and compelling theology of mission. Continuing old confusions, and new distractions and preoccupations have clouded the issue. Even the ecumenical movement tends to absorb enthusiasm that might be directly expended in world evangelism. Yet the most quoted scripture in ecumenical discussions is from Jesus' prayer "that they may all be one . . . so that the world may believe that thou has sent me." Here is unity sought for the sake of evangelical witness! The holy war against Communism becomes a substitute for the preaching of the gospel. For too many church people this war is much more exciting than witnessing for Christ; it is easier to hate Communists than it is to love men.

There are two popular philosophies today that have immobilized for many the impulse to make Christ known to the world, *existentialism* and the *theology of culture*. Existentialism focuses the individual's interest upon himself and lacks social vision. This is true even of religious existentialism. In the opposite direction the theology of culture, which reaches its most influential form in Paul Tillich, aspires to such a degree of universalism that it calls into question the compelling obligation of Christian witness. For Tillich, religion is the depth dimension of culture. His doctrine of the latent church which is present in all religions and cultures, and which is to be brought to manifestation by the reception of the New Being in Christ, seems to be a powerful support of the world mission of the church. But this philosophy, like all philosophies, is guided by a basic principle, and whether it really supports the world mission is by no means clear.

Both of these philosophies are occupied with a deeper analysis of man, and they have brought great contributions to our self-understanding. The radical question to ask is whether they constitute the ultimate answer to the problem of man, and so replace the personalism and universalism of the church. For the church has and does hold that Jesus Christ is Lord and Savior for each and every individual person. Here is particularity; the individual is not just a statistic, or a replaceable part in human society. He has a name and a place in God's design, and is the unique object of God's love. But Christ is also the Lord and Savior of all men; this is Christian universalism. Any man and every man, when he hears the gospel, can say in faith, "Christ died for me." Thus are united the particular and the universal in the direct personal relation of God to all men. We deal here with personal realities, in history and in eternity, and not with an ontology of history. The universalism of the person is not the same as a universalism of process, even if it is the process of continuous manifestation in history and beyond history of the latent church.

The theology of stewardship and mission must deal with the logic or the rational basis of Christian world mission, with its motive and with its objective. In dealing with these three elements—logic, motive, and objective—we shall not be addressing ourselves to the sceptic or the unbeliever. Naturally, those who do not believe in Christ and the Christian faith will find it difficult to justify or even to understand the passion of the church to make Christ known. We speak to the church, which is the church of Christ, and we must deal with the mission of the church as the work that Christ sends the church to do in the world, or as the work that Christ does through the church. We ourselves are stewards, the economists of this undertaking.

MASTERPLAN, MISSIONS AND MEN

The Christian mission can rightly be understood only in terms of the *purpose of God*. It is God who seeks, and sends, and saves. Both Old and New Testaments reveal this purpose and this quest of God, first for Israel and then for all men. Yahweh sent the prophets to Israel. In His name they alternately command, condemn, and comfort the unruly people that He has chosen for a great role in history. But Israel is a stubborn and stiff-necked people. They do not heed the prophets, but stone them, and ignore their summons to the service of God.

Jonah is the type and symbol of Israel, the reluctant missionary, the narrow-minded, self-centered Israelite who chides Yahweh for his compassion on the Ninevites and for His willingness to forgive them when they repent. The collision of the love of God with the hard-heartedness of His people creates an incandescent disclosure of the divine purpose in the figure of the Suffering Servant of Isaiah 53. Israel will not fit this picture of the Servant of the Lord; the great prophet of the Exile can envision what the people of Israel cannot realize.

So God sends His Son, His anointed, to carry out His purpose. Jesus saw Himself in this succession of God's sending. He tells the parable of a man who sent his servants to collect the rent of his vineyard. But the tenants "took his servants and beat one, and killed another and stoned another." At last "he sent his son, saying, they will respect my son." But the tenants said, "This is the heir; come, let us kill him and have his inheritance." So Jesus puts Himself in the line of those sent by God; His disciples saw in Him the true Servant of Yahweh, a Suffering Servant who "was bruised for our iniquities," and "with whose stripes we are healed," who gave His life in the fulfillment of His Father's purpose. His lament over Jerusalem, as He neared the end of His own earthly ministry, revealed not only a profound sorrow that all the sending of God had been met with rejection, but also His acceptance of suffering as the true Servant of God.

God's sending of the prophets, and then of His own Son reveals Him as the seeking God. It is *His* love for man, *His* purpose to redeem men, that glows in all this urgency of sending. The three parables in the fifteenth chapter of Luke's gospel furnish the three great themes of His seeking and sending; the lost coin affirms His care for the least and the lowest; the lost sheep points to the ultimate helplessness of man, and the prodigal son contains all the elements of our lostness, of repentance and return, and of the unconditional grace of God toward His wayward children. God is the Good Shepherd; God is the housewife searching for the lost penny; God is the Father rejoicing in the return of His son "who was dead and is alive, who was lost and now is found."

The seeking of God for man reached perfect clarity in Christ. Christ, then, becomes Himself the sender. God sent His Son in eternity; Christ sends His church in history on the mission of reconciliation, of service, of salvation from "meaninglessness and sin," from sin and death. He sends the church to the *world*. "World" is to be understood both in depth, and in extension. Depth means the whole life of man; extension means the life of all men. There is no corner of human existence with which Christ is not concerned, and to which He does not send His church with its message and ministry of healing. It is to the world as it actually is that Christ sends His church; in its economic striving, in its intellectual search, in the restless aspirations of its artistic spirit, in its politics and industry, in its worship and work, in its goodness and badness. A sophisticated mind might look upon this world with mingled hopelessness, disillusionment, and repulsion, as do so many dramatists and novelists today. But "God so loved the world that He gave his only begotten Son" that men might find life, and hope and fulfillment.

God sends His Son into the world of man's secular activities, as well as the world of his religious need. The church has a this-worldly, as well as an other-worldly interest and responsibility. It is itself a religious fellowship; its first witness is to the goodness and grace of God in Christ. All the world needs this "gospel." But the gospel points to the transformed and redeemed life of man in this world, in his secular existence. "Thy kingdom come, Thy will be done on earth as it is in heaven."

Extensively, the "world" means the race; all nations, all colors, all cultures, all religions. The great affirmation of this all-inclusiveness of the mission is made by St. Paul in chapters nine, ten, and eleven of his letter to the Romans. The Roman letter has been captured by the theologians for theology. Their instinct has certainly been right, for in this epistle Paul has set forth more systematically and more completely than anywhere else the doctrine and logic of the Christian faith. But we should never lose sight of the fact that he was writing primarily to provide a theological basis and justification for opening the doors of the church to the Gentile world. He was showing that not only the special Jewish world with its tradition and history finds its fulfillment in Christ, but that all men—the Gentiles— are included in the divine purpose, and have equal place and welcome in the redeemed community. In these three chapters he makes the radical shift from the limited world of the Jewish nation to the universal community of faith. Paul, like other New Testament writers, finds the key to God's purpose not in Moses and the law, but in Abraham, the man of faith. He declares that the true children of Abraham are not those who are children after the flesh, but those who are children of Abraham in faith, whether they be Jew or Gentile. The salvation that both Jew and Gentile find in Christ is through grace, not law. The righteousness of the true Israel is God's righteousness, the righteousness of faith.

The mission on which Christ sends His church is a mission both to the religious man and to the secular man; it is also to both the Christian and the non-Christian worlds. It is a mission even to the church itself, for the church in many ways is far from Christian. Perhaps never in its history has the church so generally, in all its branches, acknowledged the sin of its divisions. Under the euphonious designation of "non-theological factors" it has at least begun to confess that pride, partisanship, and spiritual blindness have a lot to do with these divisions.

We are also beginning to recognize the even greater threat to the integrity of the church that is posed by the dominance within it of the goals and standards of our secular culture, which our forefathers called "worldiness" and which we now designate "secularism."

The church for great numbers of people is important because it furnishes a religious sanction for our secular, nationalistic, and economic enterprises. Not only is the church in the world, but the world is so much in the church that it is sometimes hard to see the difference. But there is a difference. The church is the creation of God through Jesus Christ. It has His way to proclaim a way of love in the midst of the hates of men, a way of humility in the presence of pride—pride of status, pride of race, pride of personal achievement—a way of dedication to the service of men in a world where fierce rivalries and competition exalt self-interest and glorify success almost to the place of an absolute.

The church's mission is a mission to the non-Christian world in an extensive sense. Specifically, it is to all religions as well as to all races and nations. In the actual human scene these three—race, nation, and religion—cannot easily be disentangled. The greater part of the human race is still non-Christian. Most of the world lives under the dominance of religious traditions into which Christ has never come. The supreme self-revelation of God in Him is not even known. The people have conceptions of God, of man, and of human destiny that are "pre-Christian." There is much of greatness in these conceptions; there are also limitations and deficiencies that thwart the human spirit. God sent His Son for the sake of all these vast populations, just as truly as He sent Him to the people of Israel. This is the point of Paul's great treatise in the Roman letter.

But the relation of the Christian church and the Christian world to this world of non-Christian religions is not that of a "cold war." The approach of the missionary church is not a hostile, but a profoundly friendly operation. Its intention is not to condemn and discredit the great religious traditions, any more than it was the intention of St. Paul to denounce the Jewish. But it is an approach of truth, the truth of Jesus Christ. It is an evangelical operation, the heart of which is to make known God's self-revelation in Christ and to open the way to fellowship with Him, just as Paul would open the door to the Gentiles in his day.

The church's approach to the non-Christian world is one of neither theological argument nor of philosophical exchange. The earlier missionaries were often guilty of the former; they felt that the truth inhered in their theological formulas. The contemporary fallacy is opposite in temper, but similar in that it dwells within the realm of intellectual discourse. Recently, Paul Tillich, after a visit to Japan declared that "conversation not conversion" should be the way the church deals with the Buddhist, or others of non-Christian connection. Now, certainly, when two philosophers, for example, Christian and Buddhist, meet there should be conversation without any direct effort at conversion. This may be what Tillich had in mind. But the church is not a school of philosophy. It has its truths and its doctrines, some of which contradict and are contradicted by the teachings of non-Christian religions. These beliefs, or doctrines, however, are determined by the faith we have in Christ, and not by philosophical reflection. Jesus Christ is not a theological dogma, neither is He a philosophical concept. He is the historic incarnation of the eternal God, the "Event" or revelation which is given to our faith, and which must be Lord of our theology and philosophy, as well as of our hearts and wills.

No one has stated this more cogently than Paul Tillich himself:

> . . . missions is not an attempt to unite the different religions. If this were the function of mission, a uniting point, a uniting center, would have to exist. Then, however, *this* uniting center would be the center of history, and the Christ would have been decentralized.
>
> He would no longer be the center; but the center would be that which is above him and also above Buddha, Mohammed, and Confucius. The Christian church would then be *one* religious group among others, but it would not be the agency

of the kingdom of God, as we have described it and as it always felt itself to be.[1]

Unless one holds that the New Being in Christ can become the center of a people's faith and life without affecting their theology and their culture, then His coming and His acceptance as the center of history will be a conversion in the most real sense, an illumination and a recreation of the whole life of man.

TOUCHSTONES OF MOTIVATION

The motive or "occasion" of the Christian mission is the love of God moving in the hearts of Christian believers, and laying them under obligation to their fellow men. "Owe no man anything," wrote St. Paul, "but to love one another." Man as he actually is, in his lostness, his "predicament," his bewilderment, is the object of Christian love and responsibility. Here the Christian church confronts the need of man. Its responsibility lies in the fact that man without Christ does not know what he is or who he is. He may think of himself as a part of nature, or as a bit of the divine spirit entangled in flesh and lost in this world of illusion, or as a bundle of "skandhas" with no enduring reality, and subject to the relentless mathematics of *karma*. He may think of himself as a cell in the body of a clan, a caste, a race, or an economic society.

A fine humanism may see man as having certain basic needs: for food, for education, for freedom. It may cherish the ideal of full personal development, and affirm the right of every man to the realization of this ideal. And we may be thankful that such a humanism is in some degree gaining acceptance throughout the world, largely through the humanitarian pronouncements and activities of the United Nations. The rights and the needs of men as men are being acknowledged today as never before, at least in words, and many peoples are launched on the heady enterprise of claiming as their own the high if vague destiny that is implied in this humanism.

[1] "Occasional Bulletin" of the Missions Research Library, New York City, Vol. 5, No. 10, August 10, 1954.

But disillusionment and desperation are always close at hand. These high goals are ambiguous and also hard to attain. Abundance of *food*, and prosperity itself, leads to self-indulgence, vanity, bitter rivalries, and materialism. Man cannot live by bread alone, or by wealth in all of its varied forms. *Education* is good, but it can lead to pride, sophistication, and cynicism. The most bitter and frustrated people today are found among the educated. *Freedom* is a gift that more men now grasp for than at any other time in history. But freedom is most ambiguous and demanding of all. In the first place, it cannot be *given* to a people or an individual. It must be won slowly and through self-discipline, and it must be accepted as a responsibility. Freedom is a promise; it is also a threat to the peace and well-being of man. The peoples of the world, especially those of the new nations, are learning that the supreme problem of life is to know how to be free. And this is true for the individual as well as for the nation.

All these things men need and seek—food, education, freedom. But they are all ambiguous. The only unambiguous need of man is for God, and God is the only unambiguous good that man can enjoy. This is the meaning of the parables in Matthew 13. The kingdom of God, that is, God Himself, is the pearl of great price. Christ is the bread of life, He is the truth, He is the Lord in whose service man finds his true freedom. Christ reveals to man what He is and who He is. He tells every man that he is a being created in the image of God; that he is a sinner alienated from God, and therefore from himself and other men; that God the creator is his Father who loves him, and seeks him, and calls him to repentance and fellowship with Himself.

This understanding of man is difficult to attain by those who live in the traditions of other religions. It is not at all "obvious" or "natural," even when verbally it seems to be accepted. And this is the necessity of the Old Testament for the preaching of the Gospel. The Old Testament creates by the record and interpretation of history the meaning of sonship to God. The nature of that sonship develops through the experience and especially through the prophetic interpretation of the experience of Israel. It sets man before God as true personal being, free and responsible, sinful but called to repent and to return to God. It reveals the seeking love of God, and the promise of His grace. Jesus Christ comes as the embodiment and expression of this grace; He shows on the cross the cost to God of love for sinful men, and opens to all men the way of life in His kingdom. He is Himself the Son and the revelation of what sonship to God means for all men. This is the great and enduring motive of the Christian mission; it is nothing less than God's purpose to bring to men a true knowledge of themselves, and the invitation of Christ to full participation with Him in the kingdom of God.

The church is the agency in history through which God acts to bring to men the knowledge and the power of His redemptive purpose. Here is the true apostolic character of the church; its missionary character. When we speak of a missionary we usually mean a man or a woman commissioned to go to some part of the world, or of our own country, to bring the message and service of Christ. In the full meaning of the word an individual Christian cannot be the missionary; only the church itself, the actual worshipping congregation, the fellowship of faith, is the complete missionary. A person or a group of persons can be "missionaries," but in themselves they constitute only the tenuous and incomplete beginning of the full mission. The "mission" in its completeness comes when the church is formed, and when by its faith and life, its worship and service, it witnesses to the saving grace of God in Christ.

The church is the "Body of Christ." This figure of St. Paul's has been universally accepted as representing both the lordship of Christ who is the Head of the Church, and also the inner unity and the sympathetic feeling of each member for all the others. This is a glorious conception and ideal, never more than partially realized, but fundamentally true to the nature of the church. But it must not be used to justify the idea of the church as a privileged and self-contained fellowship engaged solely in seeking its own purity and enrichment. Such a "body" too easily becomes an exclusive, self-serving community anxious to preserve its high quality by bringing into its membership "the right kind of people." Not alone in racial, but also in other ways, the church often does seek to preserve its "unity and peace" by shunning all "controversial" issues. These issues today usually have to do with matters of peace or social justice. By a policy of segregation and avoidance of controversial issues the church tends to be turned in upon itself. Such a church cannot be a mission. A self-centered and protective church cannot be Christian any more than a self-centered and defensive individual can be a Christian.

The church as the Body of Christ must be true to Christ who is its Head and Heart! But the body is an organ of action, of work, and of objective relations. So the church is actually and practically the organ of Christ for the doing of His work in the world. He does in and through it His work of healing and reconciliation. It is not His church unless it is doing this work. It must not expect superficial peace and comfort, or freedom from controversy. It must strive for truth and justice and good will among men. Sometimes it must itself be "controversial." Where else can the conflicts of honest opinion, and the challenge to self-giving be made in a spirit of fairness, of humility and of charity if not in the church? The church must assume this truly Christian responsibility. It must even learn to bear the cross. For the body of Christ is placed on the cross by the sins of men, and the church cannot be the body of Christ without accepting in various ways the bearing of the cross. It is not only in Communist China, or Russia, or in Eastern Europe that this cross-bearing is required of the church, but in all lands and in all communities.

The mission of the church is a mission of both work and word. It is a false and disastrous thing to make a distinction and separation between these forms of Christian witness. The preaching of the Word has a hollow sound without the work, and the work languishes and dies without the living Word. So the church must both preach and teach, and also spend itself in service. A stronger word than "benevolence" is needed. Benevolence is good; indeed, it means good will. But the service of the church is more than good will; it is love—*agape*—and love is passionate concern not just a good intention. It stirs us out of our self-centeredness and causes us to identify our-

selves with the needy and the sinner. The Gospel does not say
that God had so much good will for the world that He sent
His Son; it says that God so loved the world. Good will would
hardly send anyone to the cross, but love does. This is the role
of the Body of Christ as the organ of God for the doing of His
work in the world.

PATHWAYS TO ULTIMATE CONCERN

The purpose or goal of the Christian mission is nothing less
than "the eternal purpose of God which He realized in Christ"
and which Christ now seeks to realize in the world. In giving
itself to this ministry the church does not commend itself. Thus
Paul wrote to the Corinthians, "For what we preach is not ourselves, but Jesus Christ as Lord, with ourselves as your servants
for Jesus' sake." The church does not "commend" its theology,
its liturgy, or a Christian culture, social ethic, or even personal
morality. For at every one of these points it is itself brought
under the judgment of Christ. It seeks however to bring the
theology, the liturgy, and culture and ethics of all religions
under the same judgment, and to bring to all men, whatever
their religion, the redemption that is in Christ.

This means that throughout human society, and throughout
the world the church in its witness will become engaged at every
point with Christian and non-Christian. There will be *conversation*. There will grow out of those conversations *convictions*
and *conversions*. Conviction means action; this is what the
church seeks in the personal and in the social life of men. Every
congregation in its own community seeks this creative change
in the lives of men. The church in the midst of a non-Christian
culture also seeks conversions. It cannot be content just to talk
about Christ; it must commend Him as Lord; it must give its
witness with the hope and prayer that the witness will create
faith.

There is, of course, an ambiguity in the term "conversion"
that needs to be clarified. It means both a vital change within
a religious faith; it also means the change to another faith.
People commonly think of conversion in the former connota-

tion; that is, the spiritual change that brings conviction, peace, and commitment. This change may take place suddenly under strong emotional stress, or it may come about through a gradual process so that the one who experiences it may not be able to say that it occurred at any one moment or in any specific act of decision. In both types of conversion, beliefs, moral purposes, and emotional life are involved; in some, one element is dominant and in others, another, but all are essentially present.

But there is also conversion from a non-Christian faith to the Christian faith. This usually takes place in those who have been for a long time engaged in relations with the Christian community, and in a "conversation" at many points affecting beliefs, moral standards, and the inner life. When anyone is in this sense converted it means that he separates himself from his inherited religious connection and becomes a part of the church, the community of Christian faith. It is because this has happened for many people in all parts of the world over a long period of time that the church is now extended into all the world, and the vision of St. Paul in some measure realized. How else could the church become a world church? It is because of such conversions that there are Christian churches in most countries worshipping God in the name of Christ, witnessing for Him, and seeking to live as members of His fellowship of faith.

But this kind of conversion is not caused by an evangelist who lays siege to the non-Christian individual and who by theological argument and emotional appeal "wins" the man to Christ. The real evangelist is the church, the local congregation when such has been created; the full missionary is present in the worship, the preaching, life, and service of a Christian community. It is this that the non-Christian "hears," and if he responds in faith and is converted, it is by action of the Holy Spirit in the freedom and secrecy of his inner life.

Such a convert inevitably will receive his Christian witness in some specific form—Protestant or Catholic; Methodist, Baptist, Presbyterian. But essentially he will not be converted to a theology, or a liturgy, or even a morality. He will be converted to Christ; he will then continue the "conversation" in ideas, morals, and worship still under the judgment of Christ and with the help of the Holy Spirit. But now he will be openly and clearly and responsibly within the fellowship where Christ is acknowledged as Lord. He will himself be a part of the Body of Christ of which Christ is the Head, and will participate in its worship and work, and in its witness to the world of the saving grace of God in Christ. He may have a conversion experience; indeed, he, like those born in a Christian home, may have more than one such experience. But this will be within the Christian community and will be the form of his personal growth as a member of the Body of Christ.

It is the mission of the church to convert all men to Christ, by its teaching and preaching, by its life and service. The missionary is the church; the power to convert is the Holy Spirit; the whole life of man is the realm of the redemptive witness and work of the church. The local congregation, in Boston or Bombay, in St. Louis or Johannesburg, is the missionary to that place. The purpose of the mission is the eternal purpose which God purposed in Christ. We are His "economists" carrying on this world-wide and age-long ministry of His love. It is required of us that we be faithful.

5

THE CHURCH AS
STEWARDSHIP AND MISSION

Frederick Herzog

Theory-building of the Christian faith requires that both stewardship and mission be viewed within the wider context of the faith. We shall seek to treat both concepts separately, examining their general human setting, their Biblical background and their present-day relevance.

THE CHURCH IS STEWARDSHIP

As an animate being man is always forced to understand himself in relationship to his environment and to nature as a whole.

Man always sought to see himself in some master-image, whether as political, rational, or tool-making animal, or as image of God. But today, more so than in any other age, does he feel the relativity of the traditional images. The increased knowledge of the various cultures has shown the historical growth of the master-images and their dependence upon contingent factors. History also in this respect has proved to be the great equalizer. Another factor to be considered is the appearance of the theory of evolution. Man, in terms of this hypothesis, sees himself as the product of a purposeless, materialistic process. Nature did not plan him. All that one might say about man is that he "is a state of matter, a form of life, a sort of animal, and a species of the Order Primates, akin nearly or remotely to all of life and indeed to all that is material" (George Gaylord Simpson). Obviously man is not very well adapted to his social responsibilities. It is conceivable that he might evolve, probably by controlling his evolution, to a being more fully adapted.

Even though man has learned that the historical views of himself are relative and that he is part of nature, he cannot avoid orienting himself in some self-image according to which he shares in the building of his culture. It is difficult to point to a comprehensive master-image that determines all our actions in society. The pluralism of our culture is too great. Perhaps it is possible to distinguish three main images that are determinative of the self-orientation of modern American man: the owner, the technician, and the waste-maker.

The present international struggle between the free world and Communism which marks all of our lives is in its root an economic battle. In brief, according to Friedrich Engels in *The Communist Manifesto*, "the theory of the Communists may be summed up in a single sentence: Abolition of private property." The view of the free world on this subject may be summarized with equal succinctness: the sacredness of private property. The West feels that man has a right to sit under his own fig tree and to count his dollars and cents which he has received in return for his own figs. Much more is involved of course: industrial production and capital and all that it implies. The basic economic philosophy, however, is simple: man is an owner, a lucky possessor of a home, a savings account, and perhaps at least a few shares in the stock market. Man is one who possesses things and whose value is mostly seen in direct proportion to his cash value.

But this is only part of the story. Man today is also a technician. Industrialization has created a mobile society. Men move from place to place as perennial transients. They find little meaning in the homes they own, which are often hardly more than minor motels to which they come for a night's rest. The farm might still be regarded as a haven of relative stability. But here, too, things have changed, especially in the relationship of the farmer to the soil. Fertilizers control the output of the land and mechanization has taken over most of the tilling and harvesting. Many farmers no longer live on the farms they own, but manage them from town.

The kind of society in which we live tempts man technically to control not only his possessions, but also his life. There is a passage of Corliss Lamont's *The Illusion of Immortality* I always considered one of the most grandiose expressions of man's desire to control his life through technology. He suggests that man eventually might "bring about a mutation which would result in a new species, Superman. It is conceivable that either man or Superman might, through science and particularly through nuclear power, gain such control over the mechanisms of this whirling planet, the solar system and the sources of energy and heat that extinction of life on this earth could be postponed indefinitely." [1] If man can control his factories, his soil and his families, why should he not be able to control his life?

The process of industrialization demands of man that he produce a never-ending stream of objects and this finally forces him to become a waste-maker. Seeking to control nature man must use it and use it fast lest his factories stand still. Vance Packard's *The Waste Makers* is a pertinent summary of the problem. Formerly, when things were out of order they were repaired. Today, says Packard, the trend is *"to encourage customers to replace particular parts rather than to bother repairing them. If the manufacturers could not persuade people to throw away the whole product and buy a new one, the next best thing was to persuade them to throw away parts."* [2] Modern men no longer have an intimate relationship to many things they own. When things seem obsolete they go the way of all waste.

From many quarters the question is raised whether man still relates himself in a really meaningful way to his environment

[1] Corliss Lamont, *The Illusion of Immortality* (New York: Philosophical Library, Inc., 1950).

[2] Vance Packard, *The Waste Makers* (New York: David McKay Co., Inc., 1960).

or whether his very desire to own, control, produce, and over-produce has not thrust the ship of his life on the vast sea of meaninglessness on which he has lost his course.

In the Old Covenant view man's relationship to nature is that of a steward.

The Bible also knows that man must relate himself to nature. Thus, beginning with Genesis we read of the mandate that distinguishes man from his fellow creatures: "The Lord God took the man and put him in the garden of Eden to till it and keep it" (Genesis 2:15). Or man's place is defined relative to the entire earth: "God said to them, 'Be fruitful and multiply, and fill the earth and subdue it; and have dominion over every living thing that moves upon the earth'" (Genesis 1:28). Man has the task of keeping and subduing, of bringing order into the raw material of nature. But more important: Man's place is understood in the context of God's ownership of his creation. God is the Lord: "The earth is the Lord's and the fulness thereof" (Psalms 24:1). With respect to his relationship to nature man can only be considered a caretaker of God's creation. The relationship between man and God in this regard is most succinctly summarized in I Chronicles 29:11.14: "All that is in the heavens is thine . . . All things come from thee, and of thy own have we given thee."

The festivals every Jew had to observe were the Feast of the Unleavened Bread, the Feast of Weeks, and the Feast of Tabernacles. At all three the Israelites were to render their thank-offerings for gifts received. God was remembered as the giver of every gift. Stewardship was properly understood: "Of thy own have we given thee." It was also understood that this offering of gifts was not merely a nice isolated gesture, but an acknowledgment of man's nature and place. Hebrew man was a warden of God's creation, a steward.

It is important to appreciate the rationale that underlies this view of man. After being told the specific requirements for the Feast of Weeks the Israelite was reminded: "You shall remember that you were a slave in Egypt" (Deuteronomy 16:12). Historically and theologically the basic factor that determined the faith of the Israelite was the emancipation of his people from serfdom in Egypt. Here Israel was established as a nation. The freedom from slavery was understood as a *gift* of Israel's God. In the light of this *gift* man's relationship to nature was defined. The God who gave freedom was also the God who gave life, in fact, life to every living thing. He was the Creator. Man depended upon Him also in his natural needs.

It is probably difficult for men who do not stand in the Jewish tradition to consider Israel's liberation from Egypt as a factor that might help to shape the master-image of human existence. Even so, they could perhaps understand that a society or people might find its center of meaning as much in an event of its past as in the compulsions of technology or science. For the Christian, however, the Exodus only foreshadows another great liberation from serfdom: the coming of God in Jesus Christ as the Savior of all people.

The church as stewardship is a response to the stewardship of Jesus Christ.

In Jesus Christ man was freed from controlling life and things. The liberation from Egypt never had led to a perfect realization of stewardship in Israel. By meticulous observance of the law the Jew still sought to control life. Time and again Israel also fell prey to the tyranny of things, money, and riches, so that Jesus had reason to emphasize: "Where your treasure is, there will your heart be also" (Matthew 6:21).

The flaw in modern man's view of himself as part of an evolutionary process is that he seeks to control the process. He must become master of his destiny as captain of industry and captain of his soul. Instead of entrusting himself to life he tries to make evolution pass into his control. The resultant tyranny of things over him is patent wherever we look.

Jesus of Nazareth embodied the opposite stance. He had no place to lay His head (Matthew 8:20). But He trusted life. He had a thankful heart: "I thank thee, Father, Lord of heaven and earth, that thou hast hidden these things from the wise and understanding and revealed them to babes" (Matthew 11:25). He knew that God cared for Him. He prayed that God's will would be done in His life. His time was in God's hands. He embodied true manhood. He was a steward of His time and talents. Stewardship was not just another role He played. It fully expressed all He was as a creature. He was a true son of God. The very fact that such a life could be lived among men was the liberation from man's attempt to control life and from the tyranny of things.

The first question perhaps that a theology of stewardship today should raise is whether contemporary man can understand himself in the light of this liberation. Jesus Christ confronts man with the expectation that he also regard himself as a steward who is thankful for the gift of life. This, of course, calls for faith and not scientific knowledge. But faith, also in this respect, is not unreasonable in view of the thousands of mentally ill who break down because of overstraining themselves in seeking to control life. There seems no reason why modern man should not understand that Jesus' attitude was sane and that it brought fulfillment of life.

Stewardship is not to be regarded as a role that man might play as a Christian besides a number of other roles. It is what comes most natural to man as God's creature. The church is stewardship insofar as she understands herself as representation of true manhood. Her major task is to reawaken man to the fundamental qualities of true manhood.

The stewardship of the Christian as an expression of discipleship relates to the neighbor as well as to God.

Jesus' stewardship included the neighbor. He spent much of His time in showing His concern for the neighbor, healing body and soul. Thus He was obedient to God. Men know themselves as stewards of God's creation in showing compassion for the neighbor. "We love, because he first loved us. If any one says, 'I love God,' and hates his brother, he is a liar; for he who does not love his brother whom he has seen, cannot love God whom he has not seen" (I John 4:19.20).

We can live meaningfully as stewards only as we break through the wall of anonymous giving and become a concrete neighbor to a concrete fellow man. Public giving in churches must continue. The news media of our denominations must continue to inform us of who the recipients of our money are. But we dare not neglect our personal responsibility in the communities in which we live. Stewardship in terms of national church programs or international missions can remain quite abstract. It relates primarily to the homes we own, the people we employ, the neighbors we live with, and our fellow townsmen on the other side of the tracks.

In Durham County, North Carolina, where I live, with a population of 112,000, the Department of Public Welfare each month since July 1961 has had at least 600 cases of permanently and totally disabled, more than 860 cases of dependent children, and more than 1,000 cases of old age assistance. Many of these "cases" live in the poorer sections of the town. As in most towns of the South, these sections are largely blighted areas with delapidated housing. The poor usually rent homes. What about a repair job, a paint job, or proper sanitation? Does the owner care? Many of the tenements seem beyond paint and repair. It is my understanding that in some areas of the town up to 90 per cent of the owners of substandard housing are church members—Negro as well as white.

In 1960 3.2-million children in the United States lived in families with incomes under $1,000 a year. Often a family cannot get away with rent less than $60 a month. This leaves little for food. At the same time church building has become a billion-dollar-a-year business. Not many of our glamorous sanctuaries are built directly with the pennies of families with an income of under $1,000 a year. But one wonders how much of the rent payments flow indirectly via the property owners into our sanctuaries. We must stress that stewardship is more comprehensive than tithing. The human soul must be reawakened, not only in the home owners, but in all walks of life. We all nod agreement when someone says that we have a responsibility for the poor beyond the Christmas baskets. But it takes imaginative thinking to discover what this practically means in the slums of our towns.

There is no point, of course, in duplicating services already rendered by the government. But Jesus sought out the needy. We, therefore, miss an important aspect of Christian living if we gear stewardship to the church only. We must get away from the pigeonhole of the pew to discover the personal aspect of stewardship.

One of the greatest challenges for our generation in my view is to find the proper balance between "institutionalized discipleship" and personal discipleship that is directly involved in the needs of a darkling world. Frank Laubach suggested years ago that each one teach one. A good mandate for our day might be: "Each one serve one." It is next to impossible to practice stewardship as a disciple of Jesus without personal involvement in suffering and need. The church as stewardship can be a company of compassion in the world. But it will take the initiative of the individual Christian to venture out on his own. In involvement with his suffering neighbor the disciple can learn that he is the caretaker of God's creation, using the things of the world to build a better community of men, a new mankind.

THE CHURCH IS MISSION[3]

Mission begins when a steward seeks to awaken stewardship in his neighbor and realizes that there is no limit to his responsibility for the neighbor.

In our last reflections we already moved into the area of mis-

---

[3] This is not a patently theocentric definition. It is understandable that today some would wish to speak of God's mission, rather than of the church as mission, since the church has often been regarded as an end in itself and mission as a means to this end. I agree with the principle implied in the view of Gerald H. Anderson in "A theocentric Approach to the Christian Mission," *The Southeast Asia Journal of Theology*, Vol. 3, No. 3, October 1961, p. 13: "The *Ecclesia* becomes the obedient servant for the *Missio Dei*. It is neither an end in itself, nor simply a means that is being used by God . . . Its function is to proclaim the Gospel (*kerygma*), and to gather those who hear and respond into loving (*agape*) fellowship (*koinonia*). The Church, therefore, exists for the mission, but is not itself the mission. Failure to make this distinction may result in an improper identification of the Church with the mission, and thereby usurp for the Church the office of God." When we speak of the *church as mission* we want to indicate, however, that she is sent to witness as Jesus Christ was sent. Cf. John 20:21: "As the Father has sent me, even so I send you."

sion. It was inevitable. One cannot speak of stewardship without touching on mission. Caretakers of God's creation, although first called upon to be responsible for limited areas of "ownership," will soon learn that they cannot escape becoming responsible for God's world as a whole.

Jesus primarily saw Himself sent to the lost sheep of Israel. His concern for men, His preaching, His works of healing, all this was directed towards His people without any special emphasis on missionary responsibility for the Samaritans or the Gentiles. But He took His stewardship seriously and He knew that it had no limits. He did not reject the request of the Syrophoenician woman (Mark 7:29) or the centurion (Matthew 8:13). In the main, however, He acted as a missionary to His people. He apparently also sent out His disciples as missionaries only to Israel.

Without getting involved in too detailed an historico-critical analysis of the Great Commission and other missionary mandates of the New Testament we must at least emphasize that for critical text analysis Mark 16:15, "Go into all the world and preach the Gospel to the whole creation," and Matthew 28:19 are additions of the primitive church. Acts and the letters of Paul clearly indicate that for a considerable period of time the apostles felt sent to Israel only and that missionary work among the Gentiles depended in large measure upon the special calling of Paul. According to Acts 1:6 the apostles were first expecting the Messianic kingdom in Israel. Peter had to be directed to establish contact with the Gentile Cornelius by special revelation (Acts 10). The initial attitude of the apostles is difficult to understand in the light of the Great Commission. The actual events do not seem to suggest that they immediately at the time of the resurrection knew the Great Commission as found in Matthew.

The vocabulary of the longer ending of Mark (16:9-20) does not agree with that of the Gospel as a whole, and the trinitarian formula of the Great Commission points to the influence of Pauline theology. The missionary mandate was most likely appended by the Gentile church, perhaps replacing a commission to call Israel to repentance. In the mandate the risen Lord is speaking, introducing the reason for the Pauline missionary endeavor presumably at a time when Israel had definitely rejected Jesus as its Messiah.

Historically the chronological detail of the Christian mission is shrouded in the mists of early Christian history. The church probably broke through its seclusion when the "great persecution arose against the church in Jerusalem" after the death of Stephen (Acts 8:1).

Whatever the exact circumstances of the common life of the first Jerusalem Christians, their communism of love as reported in Acts was a witness to the fact that the man who is newly oriented in his relationship to God understands himself as a steward and not an owner. True manhood was embodied in the life of Jesus. But the newness of life which this entailed among the disciples in Jerusalem could finally not be confined to a small group. Bursting the Jewish shell, a powerful spiritual force pressed its way into mankind. Jesus as steward awakened men to their true condition. His first disciples could not keep the newness of the human condition for themselves.

The church as mission becomes responsible for the ordering of man's communal life.

Man not only has to come to grips with nature, but also with history, the flux of human life in clans, peoples, and nations. Today two proposals of coming to terms with history stand against each other: the Marxian deterministic scheme of social evolution toward a future utopia and the capitalist vision of the possibility to experience a present utopia in material affluence. The church labors in the midst of conflicting ideologies with no promise or mandate that she can introduce the perfect order. But she understands more and more that she is the caretaker of God's creation also in the realm of man's communal existence. From the early days of the missionary movement the expansion of Christianity involved a transformation of society, first unpremeditated but later with a keen awareness of its inevitability. "The early Christian communities were not particularly concerned to transform the life of the Graeco-Roman society of their day. Yet the amazing fact is that the early Christians nevertheless made such a marked influence upon the society of their times that they were accused of fomenting social revolution (cf. Acts 17:6)" (*Twentieth Century Encyclopedia of Religious Knowledge*).

Mission will always have to evolve according to the law with which it began. It was not an attempt to blend the cultural values of Judaism with those of Greece, but the confrontation of man with his true condition: that God is already his God, claiming him as a steward. Mission was the unavoidable expansion of stewardship throughout the world. It sought to reconstruct the individual from within who, then, inevitably witnessed to his stewardship by bringing greater order to the society of which he was a part. Nevertheless, the goal of mission is not the universal state, but the kingdom of God.

The church as mission is certainly also not the attempt to unite the religions of the world in the highest possible religion. Christian mission witnesses to new manhood in Jesus Christ. Confronted with Him man is to understand himself more fully as man. This means that he is invited to experience his greatest potential in relationship to God. Mission is thus not an augmentation, but a reduction of other-worldly religiosity. It makes man concerned about the other-worldly only in relationship to his responsibility for the world in which he lives. It frees him from enslavement to things secular and cultic, and makes him use nature for God's sake.

As mission spreads it can only hope more fully to awaken men to what they already are as redeemed and justified by God.[4]

---

[4] Our essay presents the issues of stewardship and mission more in a narrative form than in the language of an ecumenical dogmatics. Theological OK words repeated time and again easily obfuscate the dynamics of our personal responsibilities. This does not mean that we are not greatly indebted to the present theological climate in our understanding of stewardship and mission. As regards God's involvement in the lives of men and history as a whole, cf. "Theological Reflections on the Missionary Task of the Church," *Bulletin of the Division of Studies of the World Council of Churches*, Vol. VII, No. 2, Autumn 1961, p. 8: "The church knows that God is at work within the events of history, and that He calls His people to participate in the struggles of life in the name of Christ, so that through their obedience—whether in partial victories or in faithful defeat —they are enabled to be signs of the ultimate victory of Christ."

Since the church cannot hope to create the ideal order, it can only offer man an order of life in which the effects of sin are less flagrant. The Christian will experience the new order of life in the sharing of suffering with his neighbor in which he re-experiences the sufferings of his Lord as He sought to awaken men to their true being. This will entail the attempt to eliminate social injustice which is a particularly flagrant cause of human suffering.[5]

The essence of the church as mission is the sharing of true manhood.

One of the most moving testimonies to the missionary commitment of present-day Christians is the story of Jim and Elisabeth Elliot. Jim was one of the five missionaries killed by the Aucas in Ecuador in 1956. They had tried to establish contact with this tribe that had never opened itself to whites before. Their airplane mission showed initial signs of success. So they landed near the Auca settlement and contacted at least three representatives of the tribe. Two days later, on January 8, 1956, they were speared by the Aucas.

Elisabeth Elliot, the wife of Jim, did not give up. She stayed in the area and learned as much as was possible of the Auca language from some Auca women who had left the tribe. About two and half years later, together with Valerie, her little daughter, and the sister of one of the five missionaries, she was able to enter the tribe that had taken the life of her husband and to live as a missionary in its midst. Reading her story in her book, *The Savage My Kinsman,* one cannot but be moved by her commitment. What makes it especially relevant to a contemporary theology of mission is the way in which she was forced to communicate the Gospel. There was very little of Christian teaching that seemed to make immediate sense to the

---

[5] *Ibid.,* p. 14: "In the missionary message itself, the Lordship of Christ over social structures and social change must be clearly proclaimed, as also this inescapable social obligation of Christian discipleship. In the contemporary world, political, social, economic and racial affairs play such a dominant part in the lives of men that the relevance of the Gospel to human life must be demonstrated in these spheres."

Aucas. About all she could do was to share life with them, the life of a primitive tribe. She writes: "In a sense, all that we did while living with the Aucas was an attempt at communication. To eat what they ate, to live in the same kind of house, to swim and fish with them, to teach them to blow up a balloon or whistle on their fingers, to learn to spin cotton thread or weave a hammock as they did, to listen hour after hour to their stories and try to write down what they said—all this was communication, the attempt to understand, to relate ourselves to them and to reach as far as possible across the chasm which separated us. Many times this seemed a naive hope. Many times I despaired of really knowing them, the secrets of their hearts. Then I realized that I did not know my own heart. In this we were one." [6]

Apparently the Aucas have no outward religious forms. They know nothing of prayer, sacrifice, worship, etc. So there was only the human level as bridge for communication. But on this level everything was at stake. The Elliots readily suffered for the Aucas and shared their life with them. Here the reality of the new manhood in Jesus Christ became concrete. It became concrete in such a way that the sharing of the Gospel was not merely giving, but also receiving.[7] Elisabeth Elliot began to understand that she was not superior as a "white" missionary. The Aucas accepted her as an equal. But this meant, for example, that she as a younger woman had to carry water for an older woman according to the custom of the tribe. In identifying with the lot of the Auca and becoming a servant she learned that the savage was her kinsman.

In identifying with the lot of the neighbor the Christian as a missionary witnesses to God's care for all men as their Creator and in serving he embodies the incarnation of God's love in

---

[6] Elisabeth Elliot, *The Savage My Kinsman* (New York: Harper & Row, 1961).
[7] *Ibid.*, p. 16: "There is a self-sufficient attitude on the part of traditionally 'giving' churches which prevents them from seeing that they must also be 'receiving' churches."

Jesus Christ.[8] Even the carrying of a pail of water for the neighbor can be an opportunity to bring Christ's spirit to bear upon the social structures of man and to witness to God's will that all men should be saved.

The church is mission only in sharing manhood in the world at home as well as the world "abroad."

Many events in the past decade have contributed to understanding that mission begins at home as charity begins at home. The reawaking of the laity has been one factor, since laymen have begun to realize that though their field of responsibility is limited, yet the mandate of awaking stewardship in the neighbor does not apply to foreign fields only.[9]

In this respect the South of the United States presents a particular missionary situation, the relationship between Negro and white, especially between Negro and white Christians. The question simply put is whether the love of God can be confined to the narrow walls of the *apartheid* in which society dwells in the South. The problem is ever with us. To talk about it means to talk about the obvious. I should not like to become wordy about it. Most of what I want to say I can share in terms of statistics.

From a study in 1959 reporting on placement by the Employ-

---

[8] As to possibilities and limits of identification with the neighbor, *ibid.*, p. 11: "While . . . it is an essential part of the strategy of mission for the Church to identify itself with men in their separate 'groupings,' in such a way that the Christian faith takes form within the particular cultural forms of their daily life, it is equally essential that the transcendent character of the Church as a supranational, supraracial and eschatological community be made clear."

[9] *Ibid.*, p. 12ff.: "The Church as the Body of Christ has a single mission. Every Christian, when he is baptized, is placed within this community of the Spirit, and receives a gift for the common good which constitutes a calling to participate in this one mission to the world . . . It should be further noted that, in a world in which new social groupings are constantly forming, and in which Christians are moving about in their secular occupations as never before, the possibilities of lay witness constitute the Church's greatest opportunity to penetrate new areas with the Gospel."

ment Security Commission in non-farm jobs in North Carolina one gets the following picture:

Category	White	Non-white
Professional, managerial	1,851	25
Clerical and sales	19,811	320
Skilled	12,824	1,315
Semi-skilled	33,609	4,241
Service	8,109	29,376
Unskilled and other	19,372	38,196
	95,576	73,473

The figures do not include those who applied directly to firms and were employed, but it does give a fairly accurate impression of employment opportunities in North Carolina.

Some might feel that there are few Negroes that could really be employed in skilled and "better" jobs. But the facts are easily to be gathered from statistics. What happens to the Negro college graduate in North Carolina? For example, Livingstone College for Negroes in Salisbury, North Carolina, had ninety-two graduates in 1960, the year the sit-ins began. Not one of these found employment in industry or business. Fifty-two became teachers (in Negro schools, of course), ten social workers, three members of the armed services, two research scientists, and twenty-five ministers and housewives.

In Durham, North Carolina, no real progress in employment practices was made until the boycotts of major stores began in 1961. By January 1962—the figures have not changed much since then—a group of thirty-one firms had let down the barriers and were altogether employing fifty-two Negroes in non-traditional jobs. That this amounted to little more than token employment is patent. But a beginning has been made.

The Negro is involved in the constant struggle of finding acceptance as a human being. A young Negro leader told me recently: "We hardly get anything from the whites unless we create a crisis—which is not favorably looked upon by many. But what else is there left for us to do?"

What is the place of the church at this point? As a denomination we may have a great missionary effort going, seeking to
tithe "mint and dill and cummin," and yet we may have neg-
lected the weightier matters of the law, "justice and mercy and
faith" (Matthew 23:23). The church's task in the South is
identification with the lot of every neighbor in the simple way
Elisabeth Elliot practiced it among the Aucas. The sharing of
God's love begins at home. Whenever we seek to confine it we
perish spiritually. The church is called to let her stewardship
"fall in line" with God's love. Newness of life shows itself in
the sharing of manhood, in suffering with the neighbor, and
working for justice wherever it is denied him.

A first concrete step towards greater stewardship could be
the desegregation of "God's lunch counter," the Lord's table,
throughout the United States, not only in the South. But here
in the South a beginning could be made. It would demonstrate
that Christians have nothing they really own or control. The
Lord's table definitely does not belong to them. It is the Lord's.

Returning into the world from the open table of the Lord,
where all would gather without discrimination, the Christian
could seek to awaken stewardship in his society and thus be a
missionary to his people. Society still must be reminded that it
has no right to make the distinctions between "mine" and
"thine" absolute. Everything society owns is a gift from God to
be shared for the benefit of all.

Mission has often been beside the point because it was understood merely as the conversion of faraway heathen and not also
as the expansion of stewardship in one's own society, as the
attempt to awaken stewardship in every neighbor. As soon as
we see our immediate responsibilities as Christians we might
better understand Jesus' strictures against meaningless "missionary" efforts overseas: "Woe to you, scribes and Pharisees,
hypocrites! for you traverse sea and land to make a single proselyte, and when he becomes a proselyte, you make him twice
as much a child of hell as yourselves" (Matthew 23:15). Awaking to our responsibility before God we might also be able to

form the proper image of ourselves and to find our place in nature: "As for me, I shall behold thy face in righteousness: I shall be satisfied, when I awake, with thy likeness" (Psalm 17:15).[10]

[10] I wish to express my appreciation to the Reverend R. L. Speaks, pastor of St. Mark A.M.E. Zion Church, and the Department of Public Welfare in Durham, North Carolina, for furnishing some of the statistics of this paper. For the data relative to Negro employment problems see the *1961 North Carolina Report on Civil Rights from the State Advisory Commission* and Gene Roberts, Jr., "Employment Problems Plentiful for the Tar Heel Negro Graduate," *Raleigh News and Observer*, September 3, 1961, pp. 1-2.

6

TREASURE IN

EARTHEN VESSELS

Roger Hazelton

Neither "stewardship" nor "mission" are Biblical words, although the figure of the steward and the image of sent-ness are of the very marrow of the Bible. To speak about the theology of stewardship and mission should mean trying to understand the church's present tasks in terms of the gospel itself. It must involve speaking a word both of judgment and mercy within and for and to the church. It must involve seeing what we already are doing in the light of what God is doing for the saving and renewing of His own world. And basically it seems therefore that the theme comes down to this: The church judged and known in its relationship to its Lord, its beliefs, it practices, its traditions in worship and teaching, its very style of life—all these judged and known in relation to the Lord of the church.

This is not as easy as it sounds. We could make theology simpler than we do, but theology is not a simple thing. And one of the curses of modern Protestanism is the bland assumption that the gospel is really very simple. It is; deceptively so. There are tricks and traps which catch the unwary when they least expect it. Therefore, it is difficult to speak about "the theology of stewardship and mission" because the gospel itself is so illusive, so haunting, and so provocative in the best sense of the word. Indeed, it is so eloquently balanced and many-faceted that it can neither be neatly packaged nor programmed in clever phraseology. The gospel has in it both a message we desire to hear and one that disturbs us. It bristles with paradox, promise, surprise, double meaning, and with God-given ambiguity.

We live in an era of the deterioration of great words. The degradation of language has reached the stage where the use of a word like "stewardship" is almost a perilous thing. In current usage the impression one gets is that stewardship means no more nor less than "giving till it hurts." When we re-examine the parables of the New Testament on stewardship, we get a completely different impression. Consider Luke 16:1-13 as an example. In this parable of the steward we encounter a real rascal. He's a middleman. He is related in two directions—to his boss, his master, and to his master's debtor. He has been squandering his master's money at a great rate, and the master has finally caught up with him and confronts him openly: "Look here, young fellow, your day is up. You are going to have to give up your stewardship because of the way you have been squandering my property." The steward pauses for some serious soul-searching. He decides that rather than go on the begging line or be shamed out of town he will work a deal with the debtors of his master. The approach follows in this vein. To the first man he inquires, "How much do you owe my master?" When given the reply, "100 bushels of wheat," he responds, "Scratch that and write down 50." Then he goes to another man and he says, "How much do you owe my master?" "One hundred barrels of oil" is the reply. Thereupon, the steward announces, "You don't any more; you only owe 80." And so on. He succeeds in collecting part of what his master's debtors owe him, but not all. His master commends him for this act. He commends him, not for his dishonesty, but for his prudence. The master says, "You know how to make friends for yourself by means of unrighteous mammon," and then adds the observation, "for the children of this world are often wiser than the children of light." That doesn't sound much like the gospel.

What really is Jesus teaching us in this parable? Clearly, the story is a paradox. He later says that you cannot serve two masters, for either you will hate the one and love the other, or love the one and hate the other. You cannot serve God and mammon. But that can hardly be the *only* moral of this story because the master has already commended the unjust and dishonest steward for making friends for himself by unrighteous mammon in the world. Jesus is emphasizing that no man can serve two masters. He said that many times. But we in our day haven't known what to do with the sons of this world who are wiser in their own generation than the sons of light. The problem does not lend itself to a simple solution. The real paradox is suggested by the question: How can I be faithful and worldly at one and the same time? How can I use mammon and not worship mammon? How can I adjust to the conditions and situations of this secular world and be mindful of my duties and responsibilities to the Master?

Finding Hidden Treasures

The necessity to face this problem arises from the fact that we had this treasure of the gospel in earthen vessels. We never have it in a pure state. It doesn't exist like H_2O in the abstract. It always exists in specific form, and one never loves and loves alone. One loves with all that clings to that love; the dross, the silt, and the rust of human sin. We never have the gospel in its purest state. To suppose we do is to live in a realm of illusion and falsehood.

We have this treasure of what God has done for us in Christ in earthen vessels. It is gift-wrapped in the printed word. It is reflected in the form and design of churches, schools, hospitals, and orphanages, and their on-going traditions. These are but an earthen vessel when compared with the treasure of the gospel.

There is much talk in our day about the real danger of a new anti-nomianism, and of a new taking-off from the realities of institutional Christianity into some radically new manifestation of religion where all is simple, clear, and unreal. There are those who speak sneeringly of religion as though its practice and institutions were essentially evil. Religion is considered by such people to be a "dirty word." They prefer to pick up Peter Berger's word "the establishment," and talk about "the establishment" with the downward curve of the lips. There is an element of truth in such critics' remarks, and there are advantages in hearing them honestly. The central consideration is to learn the difference between the container and the thing contained. Those who grasp this distinction in humility and faith can usually avoid the idolization of institution on the one hand and the impotency of unbelief on the other. We do have to understand not merely that the church is visible and invisible at one and the same time. This is its glory and its shame. But we have also to understand that the gospel itself exists nowhere, not in John 3:16 or any other place, in a pure state to which we can turn and say, "that's it." Everything else is subject to it or follows from it. No human words, not even the most inspired visions of the most dedicated and saintly man, can presume to capture within their net the meaning of the wants, the atmosphere, the weight, the specific gravity of what God has done for us in the event called Jesus Christ.

GRASPED BY THE DISCOVERY

There is a real problem to be faced. It is the problem of fidelity to that which is original with us, to that out of which we are shaped, and because of which we exist, and by which we try however poorly and haltingly to live. At the same time we must seek not merely to hold in some kind of permanent tenacity an older understanding of the gospel, but we must seek to maneuver and make flexible this understanding in all the ways and byways of human life, attempting to change the human atmosphere and climate of our world on behalf of God and Christ. The attitude of the steward is the attitude of one who holds in trust what isn't his own, and doesn't merely hang onto it, but holds it in a way that moves it toward the other for the other's good so that he becomes transmitter. He becomes mediator, middleman. He becomes one who knows who his master is and knows that by which he should be mastered, namely the gospel. But he knows that he can have no fixed or solid relationship to that gospel. Only as the gospel lays hold of him can he confront and engage on its own ground the world where God has put him to do his believing and living. Our love of the world ought to body forth God's own love of the world. Even if it cannot match it, it should reflect it in its own sphere and way. Our giving should flow out of the fact of our giftedness, or being gifted with the gospel. And this again not with propositions about what God has done in Christ, but the doing of it, the fact that it has happened to us.

SPIRITUAL MULTIPLICATION

The parable of the talents is another parable of stewardship. The moral of it is not to bury your talent in the ground but to put it out at interest where it will earn double or threefold for your master. The business of interest, of compound interest if you will, is worldly business. It's bankers' business, but it is also Christian business. The sense that we are, as John Wesley said so beautifully and clearly, "lent to be spent" is the sense of stewardship. Now, this is hard to understand today. In an era of church building, of material expansiveness and growth, it becomes extremely difficult to make the parable of the steward relevant. We might suppose that in an economy of abundance it would be easier than in an economy of scarcity to make stewardship real, but this is not necessarily so.

In time of material prosperity a church becomes introverted. It selfishly thinks of advancement and growth as the very ground of its existence. Of course, the physical church is a necessity. But sometimes there is nothing back of the church for which the church exists. There may be things out in front of the church which we all want on some other grounds, for which we might call in the church's aid. These could be good things for which we could justify our participation in the life of the church. So the church exists somehow for its own sake or for the pragmatism of our materialistic abundant, self-centered economy. It becomes introverted because it thinks about its own expansion and its own increase and its own strengthening in such a material way that the world would come and knock at its doors day after day and night after night, but the church would not be willing to listen. The church which is so concerned with its own life and its own upkeep in this way for which steward-ship is often taken as a synonym will be content with token integration, will be content with token support for theological education, will be content with token ecumenicity going on its merry introverted way all the while.

Stewardship is a two-way process. Theologically, it is possible to think of it as a reversal of the incarnation and the atonement —a rendering back to God, the Giver, of His gift with interest. Those other parables in the gospels—of the water made wine, of the man who has a feast and compels the strangers from the alleys and the slummy corners of town to come in and enjoy it —with all these curious reversals, all these odd upsettings of the normal order of decent life, really suggest something of the per-vasive meaning of stewardship to us. They all have at their heart a sense of the incredible bounty of God which overrides even men's notions of justice—of what Karl Barth likes to call God's friendliness toward man, God's favoring of man. The word for "grace" is a word which means favoring, not benig-nity, not benevolence, but friendliness on the part of the Most High toward the most low. The friendliness which does not leap like lightning across the gap in societal space to go all the way down with man, to his particular hells that he may be hounded to the center of his being for a glory of the new being which God wills for him is not worthy of the name. The gospel makes no mention of a God in isolation who issues decrees and pronouncements from on High. Rather, the gospels tell of a God who identifies Himself desperately, savingly, wholly, with man in the very crannies and interstices of his need, in the darkest possible corners of his rottenness and nastiness. They tell of a God who will not let man go out of love for man, who will be with man visiting and redeeming him, even in agony and in evil, even in darkness and in distress.

THE REINVESTMENT OF GRATITUDE

Stewardship is essentially to be discussed and understood in terms of a theology of gratitude. Gratitude is the reflection of grace, the human reflection of God's grace. What other response can there be from the man who receives undeserved, incredible, bounteous favor, except that he be grateful, surprised, astonished, and taken aback. He may indeed be shamed and brought low. But most of all, at the heart of all this many-sided experience, he will be grateful to the Giver of Grace. Think of stewardship, if you will, as a reversal of the process by which grace comes to us. It thus becomes our rendering back to God of these deeds that reflect our gratitude for that which we have received of Him. I sometimes like to think the gospel should not be translated always as Good News—but also as Good Spelled. The words mean that literally. That "spell" against the powers of darkness which is in the Word spoken by God in Christ; that undeserved eminence and lifting up of man out of the morass of his own imaginings, vanities, and entanglements; the incredible friendliness of God responded to by stewardly gratitude. We can think of the gospel as a gift which we have in trust and which, because we have it, causes us to respond in such a way that this response is essentially that of gratitude or praise or glad thanksgiving for what has been done for us and is being done for us in Christ.

An Outgoing Ingathering

When we turn to the thought of "mission" we have to shape another thought. Mission means sent-ness. It has to do with movement out from the center. The phrase which means most to me about this is: "The church exists by mission as fire exists by burning." How paradoxical is this? Would you say that fire exists by burning? Fire is consumed by burning; but the fire exists by burning, too. In the very process of its being consumed its existence is made possible. The church exists by missions as fire exists by burning. This isn't the way we have been thinking of the church, particularly when we custodians and caretakers of the establishment come together in meetings. We don't ordinarily conceive of the church as something that has to be consumed in order to exist. And yet, that's what this statement says, and it says it truly, I believe.

God is a missionary God. That's what the gospel tells us. He doesn't stay at home to receive ambassadors from the foreign country of man. He gets Himself in motion toward our desperate land on His own momentum before we even know what's the matter with us in order to win us back to Himself. The urgency of our mission in the world grows very plainly out of the urgency of the gospel itself and out of the very character of the gospel itself. The church must be "on" mission, must be "in" mission, because God is a missionary God. Today every situation is a missionary situation. We begin to get the sense of the real mission of the church, not merely by sauntering forth to do battle with demons over there in those foreign countries of ignorance and dirt, sin and unbelief. The sense of mission belongs to those humble and gentle people of God who have learned in earth's remotest corners what the church truly is. The encounter has led them to an understanding of stewardship and mission far transcending that of the condescending spiritual conqueror who goes forth armed not merely with the gospel, but with a few other goodies, like Western culture, bathtubs, and whatnot—to win the world for Christ as He said.

When we think about mission we think about sent-ness. The church is summoned and sent out of itself repeatedly. It is meant to be consumed in order that it may exist. Sometimes we put this, particularly in ecumenical literature these days, in a misleading way. References are made to a kind of a double movement or rhythm in the church's life. We speak of the gathering of the church and the scattering of the church. Then, when the speaker has said that the church must naturally be gathered in order that it may be scattered, and it gets scattered in order that it may be gathered again, he goes home and everybody is happy. It isn't quite enough. There is more than rhythm here. The church exists by mission as fire exists by burning. The church cannot live by a double process whereby on Sundays it is gathered and on Wednesdays or Fridays it is scattered. What we are saying is that it is one in its scattering. The church is consumed in order that it may exist, and it exists in order that it may be consumed. To speak of the mission of the church is to speak of that self-giving, of the very structures and institutions of religiousness themselves which have to be bent and sometimes broken in the service of the world in order that they may be approved of God.

Another thought which needs to be clarified in relation to mission is that of the unity of the church. It was, of course, the experience of missionaries which provided the first impulse for the ecumenical movement. The missionary meeting at Jerusalem in 1910 was really the first of the ecumenical world meetings. One could easily see why this could be so. In the overseas situation the denominational enterprise looks a little ridiculous, and if you have ever talked to a North Korean Southern Baptist, you know why. Bishop Gibson of the Protestant Episcopal Church in Virginia reported to an ecumenical gathering that when the Protestant Episcopal missionaries went into China they tried to translate into Chinese the phrase "Protestant Episcopal Church" and found some difficulty. Finally they came up with this translation, "The Church of the Kicking Overseers." It isn't merely the amusing and ridiculous aspect, but the incredible waste and the stodginess and the smugness that should concern us. A taxi driver in New Delhi took me past a great palatial home and he said in broken English, "Do you see that house?" And when I said, "Yes," he said, "That's where the Methodist Bishop lives. It's bigger than the Prime Minister's palace." There are other reasons why the ecumenical impulse came first from the mission fields and we need not relate them here. But I'm trying to make the simple point that the relationship between unity in the church and the mission of the church is very, very close and very, very real.

RECOVERY OF VISION AND ADVENTURE

Now in all this matter of mission I feel we have another paradox. In terms of mission—that church is most itself when it is least itself. We talk much about the "establishment" of the church with a certain cynical tone. Surely our feeling of cynicism and despair at this point is due to our profound suspicion that the church will not change, and that the church confronted by the unbelievable demands of the world for flexibility and mobility of mission, for imaginativeness and daring in mission, will choose to stand pat. But if the church is most itself when it is least itself, it doesn't need to be afraid of the coffeehouse church, of the industrial mission, of the store front, of the lay retreat center, of the academy. It doesn't need to be afraid of these things. Because the church which knows this about itself will know that it cannot anywhere draw the line between itself and the world with finality, with accuracy, with condescension. It knows that the claims for new forms of the church, which may not look very churchly at first, are definitely before us all.

The message and the mission of the church are one. They are one thing, not two. It isn't as if we had over here a proclamation to deliver and over there a service to perform. The meaning of "faith" is that the performing and the serving, the proclaiming and the serving, are one, and the word and the act are one. As they are one in the aboriginal shaping act of our community of faith, that by which we come into being and for which we exist, so they are one in every act or every decision of our own. What we are speaks more loudly than what we say. The proclamation of the gospel that really matters and counts for most is that service which is rendered in and for the world by the church.

Now, this mission and this message, this word and this act, which are essentially bound up with each other when proclaimed, come in another strange way. They come with the accent of servanthood and humility and self-emptying upon them. But they also come with the ring of a transcendent authority. One of the strangest things is the way in which in the gospel the figure of Jesus our Lord is constantly thrown against the screen of our thought, our imagination, our faith, in the unmistakable image of One who is both Servant and Master. If there were a reason for our intruding upon the pleasant, comfortable life of folk who don't want to hear the gospel, if we were asked why we should intrude upon their we're-very-happy-thank-you sort of existence, the answer is: we don't. God has already intruded in Jesus. He is a missionary God. The intrusion has already been made. The interference with the tenor of man's blasphemy, irony, idolatry, and grief and self-fomented sin has already happened. We are not intruders. We are proclaimers and renderers of the gospel. "What we preach is not ourselves but Jesus Christ as Lord with ourselves as your servants for Jesus' sake." Our proclamation and our service are one thing even as the Word and "act" of God in Christ is one thing.

This rhythm about the church's life which often looks like an alternating current of one sort or another is not as rhythmic as may at first appear. It is in its work that the church worships God, too, and it is in its worship that the church does that which God has given it to do. Some mission is outreach. Some mission is offering. And, as in any deep and profound relationship involving human beings with each other, it is very difficult to say where giving ends and receiving begins. A young person who was having trouble with his lady love came to talk to me about it. He made a safe observation. He said when you really love someone it is not too clear whether you are giving or taking, because the relationship is so firm it isn't always clear what comes from whom or what goes out to whom. I think it is the same in the life of faith. Our ministry is sometimes outreach, sometimes offering, sometimes work, sometimes worship. But unless the work has the accent of worship, of liturgy, of sacrifice, then we really haven't understood the business of mission and the business of ministry at all.

THE SERVANT: IMAGE AND REALITY

All this can be summarized in a fairly plausible and not too over-simple fashion. The form of the church, the shape of the church, its style of life for our time, is the form of the servant Lord. We are not asked to take orders from Him or to emulate Him at a distance. We are simply asked to do what He does and because He does it and as He does it. We are asked to be servants in our time and place within the sphere of our competence and the sector of our responsibility.

When the New Testament refers to "servant," two words are used. One of these is the word for slave. That's a very demeaning word. It refers to the status of the servant as one who always gives place to another, who seeks the lowest place, who is a used person—that is, of use to others. The other word which we are only beginning to explore in the church with the depth that we should is the word deacon. The servant is the deacon. Deacon refers not to the status of the servant, but to his functions. Now "service" like "stewardship" is an almost impossible word. We have "service" stations. We have curb "service." We have "service" clubs. We have all kinds of enterprises referring to their function as a "service." When this word is used in the context of our faith, we naturally find it disenchanted. But think of servant primarily in terms of the figure of the Christ who emptied Himself, becoming one with us, that He might restore us to fellowship with His Father. Think of servanthood as identification, as bending our life into the shape of another man's need. Think of servanthood not as humiliation, but humility. Humility does not require the meaningless acceptance of self-depreciation. Rather, it is the full and unrestrained submission of oneself to God, in relationship of prayer, trust, hope, believing, faith, and love.

Servanthood, then, takes the form, stance, and style of life assumed by our Lord Himself as He came to visit and redeem His people. Stewardship and mission must come together in the form of a servant, so that stewardship is not doling out and mission is not giving from an eminence to a depth, but becomes that beggar-like condition of which D. T. Niles speaks where one beggar tells another where he might get food. Until stewardship and mission become alike in the form of a servant, and until the form of the servant becomes the form of the church, we shall be a long, long way, not merely from understanding the meaning of these words and their theology, but from entering in any degree at all into the reality to which they point us.

7

EVANGELISM:

THE PURPOSE

OF STEWARDSHIP IN MISSION

Winburn T. Thomas

Since stewardship is always a matter of the Christian doing the will of his Lord, the Christian's prime responsibility is to discover the purposes of God. The New Testament teaches that the will of God is to bring all men into a loving relationship with their Father. The mission of the church is to evangelize, to spread this good news. Historically, the stewardship movement is rooted in the need for funds to carry out the mission of the church. It is appropriate to study "mission and evangelism" as a basis for stewardship.

What Is an Apostle?

The New Testament appears to make no clear-cut distinction between apostle (*apostolos*) and evangelist (*euaggelistes*, from *euaggelizomai*, to bring the good news). Herodotus refers to a messenger sent forth to arrange a truce as "the apostle." The New Testament (John 13:16, II Corinthians 8:23, Philippians 2:25) uses the term rarely to mean "he that is sent." The gospels use "apostle" exclusively to refer to the original Twelve. Paul usually means by the term, "apostle of Jesus Christ" (I Corinthians 15:3), and used it to refer to himself. The New Testament sets out no test for apostleship, or the qualifications required. Romans 16:7 indicates that Andronicus and Junias were apostles; and Galatians 1:10 intimates that James, the brother of Jesus, was an apostle. According to I Corinthians 12:28 ff. and Ephesians 4:11, the apostle held the highest office in the church (followed by prophets, teachers, and miracle workers). Paul adduces his having seen the Lord (I Corinthians 9:1) as proof of his apostleship, but the Church (Acts 1:23ff., Galatians 1:15ff.) set apart Matthias, then Paul and Barnabas, the Holy Spirit first having designated them as apostles.

Paul's definition of an apostle is one whose work is to preach Christ (Galatians 1:16) and the gospel (I Corinthians 1:17) to those who have not heard it. Yet, while Silvanus and Timothy were associated with Paul in preaching the gospel at Corinth (II Corinthians 1:19) neither is called an apostle (II Corinthians 1:1, Philippians 1:1, Romans 16:21).

More recent Biblical research has gone back to the Hebrew to understand the Jewish conception of *apostolos*. The Hebrew equivalent *shaliach* connotes one who is empowered to engage in a specific mission or to speak in the name of him who sends, and therefore a plenipotentiary. Christ sent out His disciples as apostles, but upon their return, they reverted to their status as disciples. Only following Pentecost was their apostolic mandate made permanent. After Paul, the early Church restricted the term *apostle* to him and the Twelve. Revelation 21:24 mentions the "twelve apostles of the Lamb" as though they were the only apostles.

Conclusion: Apostles are men appointed and sent by Christ with a mandate and authority to continue His ministry. (John 21:21, "As the Father has sent me, even so send I you.") Alan Richardson says "They bear witness to the facts of the Gospel; they teach, give decisions on discipline, and provide for the needs of the expanding church by 'sending' other ministers." [1] *Apostle* connotes *mission*, that is, being sent to continue and participate in that movement of God towards man which began with the sending of Christ and the Holy Spirit (Acts 13:4, I Peter 1:12).

[1] A *Theological Word Book of the Bible* (London: S.C.M. Press; New York: The Macmillan Co., 1950), p. 146.

FUNCTIONS OF AN APOSTLE

The New Testament function of the minister is as "one who serves" (*diakonos*) and one who "provides oversight" (*episcopos*). All the ministerial functions are gifts of grace (*charismata*). The listing of apostles, prophets, and teachers in I Corinthians 12:28 is not an hierarchical enumeration of ecclesiastical offices, but of the variety of functions which contribute to the church's corporate life arising from the diverse operation of the One Spirit. One man might exercise all these functions, as Paul did.[2]

I Corinthians 12:28 separates the functions of apostle from prophet and teacher. The apostle as preacher proclaimed the coming, death, and resurrection with a view to creating or strengthening belief. The prophet renewed and deepened conviction, repentance, and hope. The teacher provided constant instruction in the practical duties of the Christian life, grounded them in the scriptures, and dealt with problems raised by Christian belief. (A college dictionary defines an evangelist as "one of a class of teachers in the early church, next in rank after apostles and prophets." Yet the evangelist was concerned with the *Kerugma*, not with the *Didache*. The dictionary also errs in using the term "rank" rather than "function," if Richardson's distinction stated in the conclusion of part I above is correct.)

Ephesians 4:7-12 adds evangelist to the I Corinthians 12:28 list of functions. Philip (Acts 21:8) is an evangelist. Ephesians refers to traveling evangelists set forth in I Corinthians 12:28 as having a different function than an apostle, as in Acts 8, where the apostles came down to Samaria to complete the work begun by Philip. The function of the evangelist is to preach the *euangelion*, the good news of the gospel in Christ.

Alan Richardson summarizes thus: "The Church did not begin as an undifferentiated mass of believers, and then produce its own ministry for itself; it grew as a body around the

[2] *Ibid.*, pp. 146-147.

apostles whose position was determined by the act of the historical Christ. They then 'sent' other ministers to carry forward their work and similarly to teach with authority in the name of Christ." [3]

Evangelization is *euangelizesthai* (to preach good tidings), *katangellein* (to declare, announce), and *kerussein* (to proclaim as a herald), i.e., the telling of news to people who had not heard it before. New Testament preaching is not directed to the converted, but is the proclamation of the "good tidings" to the non-Christian world. The *kerugma* ("thing preached," "proclamation") was the possession of the Apostolic church. Early apostles, then evangelists, went out with this *kerugma*. In Peter's preaching the *kerugma* connotes six elements:

1. The age of fulfillment, the latter days foretold by the prophets, has dawned.
2. This has taken place through the life, death, and resurrection of Jesus; the evidences of His Messiahship are recounted; spiritual prophecy is fulfilled.
3. By virtue of the resurrection, Jesus has been exalted to the right hand of God as the Messianic head of the New Israel.
4. The Holy Spirit in the Church is the sign of God's present power and glory.
5. The Messianic Age will shortly reach its consummation in the return of Christ.
6. An appeal is made for repentance; forgiveness is offered; the Holy Spirit and salvation are promised.[4]

ROLE OF THE EVANGELIST

Bishop J. B. Thoburn of India, addressing the Ecumenical Missionary Conference,[5] limited the term *evangelist*, on the

[3] *Ibid.*, p. 151.
[4] C. H. Dodd, *The Apostolic Preaching* (London: Hodder and Stoughton, Ltd., 1936), pp. 171-172.
[5] *Ecumenical Missionary Conference in New York 1900*, Vol. II, American Tract Society (New York, 1900) p. 106ff.

basis of Philip's activity, to men who preach Christ with power sent down from heaven. He would exclude the itinerants, such as Africa's Livingston or the missionaries who move from village to village. Despite Thoburn's clear distinction, the conference discovered, as D. T. Niles has put it, "Evangelism is like ivory hunting; the elephant tusk usually is attached to an elephant." So the conference discussed the physician[6] and the teacher[7] as evangelists; under "Evangelistic Agencies" it includes education, literature, medical missions, personal work, and philanthropy. Evangelism at the turn of the century was interpreted to include the whole gamut of missionary activities.

Dr. Charles R. Erdman, one-time Professor at the Princeton Theological Seminary, in his contribution to the Mott-edited symposium on evangelism says: "In the New Testament, the work of an evangelist was specifically that of a foreign missionary. . . . The term evangelism, therefore, is properly used in reference to proclaiming the Gospel Message either at home or abroad." [8]

D. T. Niles, in his *The Preacher's Task and the Stone of Stumbling*,[9] states the chief problem of evangelism "is the problem of knowing how and when to harvest" for the real Evangelist is Christ. Yet, paradoxically, Niles immediately cites Hebrews 3:1, He is the "apostle and high priest of our confession." In addition to being proclamation, Niles says, evangelism is also prolepsis—the use of a term in anticipation of its becoming applicable—that is, those who have not yet confessed Jesus to whom the gospel is proclaimed, already are within the love of Jesus.

John R. Mott, in his Sam P. Jones Lectures at Emory University in 1944, uses the term "The Larger Evangelism" to refer to the church's necessary missionary response to the world situation. For instance, he says, "it is the obligation of the

[6] *Ibid.*, pp. 188-195.
[7] *Ibid.*, pp. 118-121.
[8] John R. Mott, ed., *Evangelism: Its Meaning* (New York: Harper & Row, 1938), p. 92.
[9] (New York: Harper & Row, 1958), pp. 108-112.

Church to evangelize the world in this generation because all men need Christ and the need is indescribably great."[10] Referring to the wide varieties of methods employed by great names of the church in education, health, preaching, writing, etc., he concludes, "It is possible to evangelize the world in view of what world missions has achieved." [11]

A standard college dictionary gives "evangelist" these varied meanings: (a) a preacher of the Gospel, (b) a revivalist, (c) an occasional or itinerant preacher. A "missionary," however, is (a) a person sent to work for the propagation of his religious faith in a heathen land or a newly settled district, (b) any propagandist, (c) one sent on a mission. The same dictionary under the term "apostle" limits the missionary implications to the Twelve.

The distinction which our age has drawn between missionary and evangelist is pragmatic: the "missionary" is one who is sent to establish his religion among non-believers, while the "evangelist" preaches generally to Christians, a task more akin to the teachers in the early church.

EVANGELISM AS MISSION

Yet this distinction can be applied only generally. "Mission" and "missionary" have become secularized. Doolittle led a bombing "mission" over Tokyo. AID is the overseas developmental "mission" of the United States government. The Peace Corps is referred to in "missionary" terms. A columnist has asked for "missionary" zeal among the inhabitants of the emerging nations that they so develop as to retain their freedom. If the churches have been anxious to dispense with the term "foreign missions," national and international governmental bodies have been quick to appropriate it.

Within the church, likewise, the term "mission" is used in several confusing senses. The "local mission" and "general mis-

[10] John R. Mott, op. cit., p. 82.
[11] Ibid., p. 87.

sion" of the United Presbyterian Church refer to programs. "Ministry," "stewardship," and "evangelism," are used interchangeably with and as synonyms of "mission."

The term "evangelism," in turn, has bad connotations because it has been used synonymously with "revivalism" and "proselytism." Dr. Elmer Homrighausen distinguishes between five kinds of "evangelism": (1) taking the gospel to the non-Christian with a desire to have him accept it; (2) an evangelizing anew of the saints; (3) the nurture of baptized children; (4) the Christianizing of the churches, which are filled with nominal believers who have not accepted the mission of Christ; and (5) a goad to and characteristic of the other ministries of the church.[12]

The National Council of Churches has developed this definition of "evangelism": The presentation or proclamation of the Good News of God in Jesus Christ in the power of the Holy Spirit, so that men will put their trust in God through Him, confess Him as Savior from the guilt and power of sin, acknowledge Him as Lord in the fellowship of the Church, and serve Him as King in all the vocations of the common life.

In contrast, mission essentially is "a word of movement, denoting the outreaching responsibility of the Church towards those in every land who do not know the name of Christ, or who, knowing it, have not confessed it." [13]

Bishop Lesslie Newbigin[14] introduces his definition of *mission* with Luke 4:18-19 in which Jesus quotes from Isaiah 61:1-2.

> The spirit of the Lord is upon me because he has anointed me;
> He has sent me to announce good news to the poor,
> To proclaim release for prisoners and recovery of sight for the blind;

---

[12] Elmer Homrighausen, *The Ecumenical Era in Church and Society*, Edward J. Jurji, ed. (New York: The Macmillan Company, 1959), pp. 214-227.

[13] Norman Goodall, *ibid.*, p. 108.

[14] *One Body, One Gospel, One World*. International Missionary Council, (London, 1959), p. 17.

To let the broken victims go free
To proclaim the year of the Lord's favor.[15]

Yet Clement C. Chesterman, M.D., Secretary of the Baptist Missionary Society, London, and former missionary in the Belgian Congo, when asked by Dr. John R. Mott how he would define evangelism, replied, "As Jesus did in his autobiography," then proceeded to quote this same passage, indicating the spiritual, social, medical, and political elements involved.[16] Newbigin refers to these same elements as the mission program of Jesus, the execution of which the New Testament records.

Many of the other contributors to Dr. Mott's symposium confuse the two terms similarly. Dr. Julio Navarro Monzo, a Brazilian publicist writes "instead of using the word evangelism I should prefer to use the term apostolate . . . I have always believed that the second word corresponded to whatever influence I was exerting." [17]

Newbigin sharply distinguishes between mission and evangelism (and disagrees explicitly with publicist Monzo) in his pamphlet quoted above: "Evangelism is an activity of the mouth or pen by which the good news of God's redeeming acts is communicated . . . Each of these two activities (evangelism and service) has its proper dignity within the wholeness of the mission, and neither should be subordinated to the other . . . nor should they be separated." [18] Yet the Bishop has not been completely consistent in observing this distinction. His address to the Bangkok Conference in December 1949, on "The Christian Challenge," sets forth the germ distinction found in his later pamphlet *One God, One World, One Mission:* "The Church is not the Church in any New Testament sense unless it *is* a mission . . . All the varied Christian activities both of witness and of service mutually complement and strengthen one another, because they all visibly proceed from the same

[15] *The New English Bible.* © 1961 by the Delegates of the Oxford University Press, and the Syndics of the Cambridge University Press.
[16] Mott, *op. cit.,* p. 80.
[17] *Ibid.,* p. 65.
[18] Newbigin, *op. cit.,* p. 22.

source, which is the Church." [19] Yet later in the same address, discussing the part played by the foreign missionary enterprise in the spiritual life of the younger churches, he speaks of the church of South India having "been given a small share in the evangelization of Pauua," thus using missionary activity and evangelization interchangeably, as did the slogan of the Student Volunteer Movement: "The evangelization of the world in this generation."

Thus Europe and North America are mission field in exactly the same way as Africa, Asia, and Latin America: continents full of men who need the gospel of Jesus Christ. The stewardship of that Gospel is the responsibility of Christians everywhere.

[19] The Christian Prospect in Eastern Asia (New York: Friendship Press, 1950), p. 83.

8

STEWARDSHIP IN

HOME MISSIONS[1]

T. K. Thompson

A definition of the term "stewardship" is difficult. The *Oxford Dictionary* maintains that the origin is the word *stye* meaning "hall," whereas *Webster's Dictionary* states that the origin is *stig* meaning "an enclosure for livestock." The word "steward" therefore denotes a person in charge of either a hall or pigsty. In its derived English usages the word has come to mean any person who cares for the property of another. In its wider ramifications it means a person who exercises an authority or a commission from a higher realm. The two Greek words in the New Testament that are commonly translated as "steward" are *oikonomos* and *epitropos* (only in Matthew 20:8). It is significant to note that there is no exact equivalent of these words in English, German, or French. Indeed, the researches of Dr. John Reumann[2] indicate that the meaning of *oikonomos* greatly changed over a usage period of 800 years. The word may refer to a priest in the mystery religions, a treasurer, an estate manager, a public official, secretary, or comptroller.

[1] A condensation of a study prepared for the World Council of Churches on Christian Stewardship, 1961.
[2] John Reumann, *The Use of Oikonomia and Related Terms in Greek Sources to About AD 100 as a Background for Patrist Applications*, University Microfilms, Ann Arbor, Michigan.

The fundamental idea, however, is clear from its etymology: *oikos*, "house," and *nomos*, "law." Therefore, the root meaning is "a person who administers the running of the house."

Oikonomos is transliterated into the English "economist." The original meaning "house economist" expanded to include the whole order of buying and selling, getting and spending by the individual, the family, and the whole world. As the ordering of time and talent on the basis of a value system also is involved, the word has come to include "vocation," that is, the means whereby a person earns his living and also by which he expresses his philosophy of life.

The root meaning of *oikonomos* has been broadened to include so much that it is virtually meaningless. This tendency is noted in the definition of Dr. Walton H. Greever who defined stewardship as "the practice of the Christian religion." [3]

The standard definition used in American Protestantism for the past fifteen years is as follows: "Christian stewardship is the practice of systematic and proportionate giving of time, abilities, and material possessions, based upon the conviction that these are trusts from God to be used in His service for the benefit of all mankind in grateful acknowledgment of Christ's redeeming love." (Constitution, National Council of Churches.)

However, this definition has been criticized widely in recent years because it limits stewardship principally to giving. A committee is actively restudying the definition, but it is too early to report on their conclusions. I therefore suggest the following interim definition:

Christian stewardship is man's complete and joyful obedience to God who entrusts to him the management of life and possessions that the world may know Jesus Christ as Lord and Saviour.

This definition embraces the three fundamental ideas of stewardship: (1) the responsible individual or group; (2) a definite entrustment from a higher authority; and (3) an ultimate accounting to that Supreme Power.

---

[3] Walton H. Greever, *The Work of the Lord* (Westwood, N.J.: Fleming H. Revell, 1937) p. 62.

For our present purposes, we are considering the history of
Christian stewardship in North America, including Canadian
Protestantism, but excluding the Roman Catholic Church and
Jewish organizations. While these non-Protestant groups have
worthy stewardship traditions, they are not comprehended
within the limits of this chapter.

HISTORICAL FACTORS

At the risk of over-simplification, I suggest the following historical divisions: (a) the colonial period, 1607-1776; (b) the
frontier period, 1776-1860; (c) the industrial period, 1860-1914;
and (d) the modern period, 1914-present.

The Colonial Period, 1607-1776

Much idealism has been written into the history of the American colonies. While the Congregationalists in New England
desired their own particular form of religious organization, and
the Quakers in Pennsylvania and the Roman Catholics in Maryland wanted political freedom, the basic reason for establishing
the new colonies was economic. By the seventeenth century
there was little additional land in Europe available for agricul-
ture. Until the Industrial Revolution Europe had to export its
surplus population, which it did with much vigor during the
seventeenth, eighteenth, and early nineteenth centuries.

The fact that the colonists did not come to North America
for purposes of religious freedom is easily demonstrated, in the
establishments of the Anglicans in Virginia, the Congregationalists in New England, and the Reformed in New Amsterdam.
Real religious liberty existed only on the Baptist Plantation at
Rhode Island, in the Quaker colony in Pennsylvania, and in
Lord Baltimore's Catholic colony of Maryland. With the forma-
tion of the United States the only practical compromise was a
Constitutional separation of church and state. Thomas Jeffer-
son and many of his colleagues subscribed to a vague sort of
deism which was consistent with this pattern. Some forms of
establishment remained in New England until 1833, but the
Constitution made for *voluntary* support of the churches. The

stewardship consequences were immediate and far-reaching. Citizens could have a church only if they voluntarily banded themselves together and assumed financial responsibility.

The Frontier Period, 1776-1860

In 1776 only on the Eastern Seaboard was there a settled, stable society. About 100 miles to the west the frontier began. There were settlements at key junctures of rivers, like Fort Pitt, later to be known as Pittsburgh, and St. Louis, a French fur-trading post at the juncture of the Missouri and Mississippi rivers, but the vast reaches of the continent lay untouched. As the emigrants moved westward certain characteristics emerged which conditioned the developing churches.

Isolation The North American continent was relatively unpeopled. Anthropologists are agreed that not more than a million Indians inhabited the area now known as the United States and Canada. Though great injustice was done to these aborigines by the white settlers, the continent was for the most part unpeopled. The basic condition of the pioneer social situation was isolation.

The land-hungry immigrants from Europe cut the forests, cleared the fields, and laid claim to vast acreages which they hoped to develop. Whereas European farmers lived in villages and worked in distant fields, North Americans lived on the land, in isolated one-family dwellings, going to the nearest settlement only on market days or perhaps on worship days.

Under such conditions a settled ministry was impossible. The classic picture of Bishop Francis Asbury, reading on horseback, following the tradition of John Wesley in England, was true not only of Methodist preachers, but of all ministers. At annual or semi-annual "revival meetings," with the same pastor preaching every evening for two weeks, people received their religion in concentrated doses. Many of the preachers or revivalists had little or no formal training and in many cases their library consisted solely of their Bibles.

In the absence of a settled clergy the preaching, teaching, baptizing, and burying of the dead was performed by lay leaders, farmers with or without formal orders. Under the conditions of the frontier the ideal preacher was the "ordained layman." The frontier minister had to be strong physically, be able to travel formidable distances, accept what hospitality was offered, live for long periods without the comforts of home, talk with the farmers about markets, crops, and weather. He had to preach without notes, expound the Bible with vigor, spice his sermons with humor and everyday human-interest stories. The village congregations feared and hated the big cities back East with their culture, their financial dominance, and their political controls. The highly educated, full-time, professional clergyman found little welcome on the frontier.

The barter economy   The visiting clergyman was more often paid in tobacco, whisky, and "keep" than in cash. Little money of any kind was exchanged. The farmer brought his eggs and produce in from the farm and traded at the country store for coffee, sugar, and gunpowder. The log cabin churches were built by volunteer labor, and the ministers were paid largely in "kind" and in services performed by the community. These conditions obtained for much of the country west of the Alleghany Mountains until the time of the War Between the States.

The unsalaried clergy   Under primitive economic conditions it was not possible to guarantee the minister a specific dollar salary. He would certainly have a roof over his head and enough to wear and eat. Frequently, a resident clergyman would be furnished acreage which he himself could farm to furnish his table. His skill as an agriculturist enhanced his status in the community. On the frontier it was difficult to think of the ordained clergyman as different from the other farmers. He usually had little formal education and his ability for expounding the Bible was usually self-taught. The Congregationalists, Presbyterians, and Anglicans, who insisted on higher educational standards for all clergy, were soon outnumbered by the Baptists, Disciples, and Methodists, who would ordain any man who felt he had a "call."

"Voluntary association"   Alexis de Tocqueville, in the 1830s, characterized American society as abounding in voluntary associations. Any ideal was apt to attract a group of citizens who organized themselves and promoted the cause. The genius of

the frontier was that any group of people could band together
for any purpose. The Constitutional requirement of the separation of church and state meant that religious societies were no
different from the secular. The principle of pluralism was accepted as a matter of course.

*Congregational polity as the ecclesiastical form of voluntary
association* Church historians have observed that by whatever
name, congregational polity is the dominant pattern of American churches. Bishops and presbyteries have had great difficulty
in exercising discipline over their congregations. On the frontier
any kind of central authority, governmental or ecclesiastical,
was suspect and disliked. Congregational polity seemed to be
more democratic and more representative of the differing points
of view. A dispute or split within the congregation was almost
certain to eventuate in a new congregation, and when these
splits took place on the national level a new denomination developed. With plenty of land and a rapidly increasing population there seemed to be an ever-growing "market" for new
denominations and new churches.

*The development of missionary giving out of the two great
awakenings of the eighteenth century* During all of the eighteenth century, and for thirty to forty years into the nineteenth,
the emphasis was upon home missions, especially the development of the West. In 1810, however, the American Board of
Commissioners for Foreign Missions came into being and the
foreign mission enterprise of North America was born. Luther
Rice returned from India to help organize the Baptist movement in the South and Southwest, primarily as a means of sup-
porting Adoniram Judson, his foreign mission colleague. At
first missionary collections were difficult because most trade was
by barter, but as the country moved toward a money economy
during the nineteenth century missionary offerings became easier to transmit.

Many of the larger Protestant denominations of North America developed formal structures to administer and channel
missionary operations at home and abroad. The development
of the stewardship movement was stimulated by the necessity
of raising large missionary budgets with which to finance the

world-wide work of the churches. Voluntary stewardship in the United States and Canada therefore stands in contrast to the tax-supported church of northern Europe. Whereas on the continent missions were supported by voluntary offerings, the home base was generally supported by taxation. Missionary giving in Europe tended to be an elective of the few, but in North America the total denominational enterprise was supported by the voluntary giving of the entire congregation.

By 1860 much of the United States and eastern Canada had been covered with a network of railroads. The travel hardships of the frontier were largely, though not completely, past. With the outbreak of the War Between the States over the questions of states' rights and slavery a new period of industrial growth began.

The Industrial Period, 1860-1914

The factory method of production The first mark of industrialization was the factory method of production. Assembly lines were introduced and with the advent of good railroad facilities there was a constant supply of raw materials and finished merchandise. Machines of many types were patented and America began to change from an agricultural to an industrial nation.

The cash economy A second mark of the industrial period was the cash economy. On the frontier each family wove its own cloth, stored its own food, and was virtually sufficient unto itself. With the development of better transportation and communication the frontier agricultural community moved rapidly toward the selling of cash crops and the buying of factory-made clothes, tools, and luxuries. With the population growth of urban areas a ready cash market was available for agricultural produce and, in turn, the farmers were able to purchase necessities and luxuries from the cities. At first in the cities, then more slowly through the country, church offerings began to be made in cash rather than in "kind," and the paid clergy began to replace the farmer-preacher.

World involvement The frontiersman shared the first President's desire to avoid "entangling foreign alliances." Increasingly, however, the American found isolation difficult to maintain. He was able to sell cotton and tobacco to Europe. Industrial New England was buying many of the food and fiber products of the Midwestern farm. The War Between the States demonstrated the world involvement on the economic level. The Mexican and Spanish-American wars threatened the isolationism of the frontier agriculturist.

A movement for world missions grew rapidly after 1810 and it was not long until every denomination had its foreign mission board. In some communions the peak of foreign missionary giving occurred between 1870 and 1890. In 1871 the Congregationalists gave more for missions than they expended locally.

The growth of central government The federal government grew in power and influence after the War Between the States. The spark that started the war was states' rights. The economic value of slaves dictated the necessity for the slave states opposing the federal government. The victory of the North meant that the Union was forcibly maintained. The country thereafter moved rapidly toward a national culture, thus overcoming the implicit regionalism in the Southern secession. Ecclesiastically, this meant that many denominations were organized on a national basis and to a degree partook of the nature of a central government.

By 1914 the main lines of American economic and political culture were clear. America was fast becoming an industrial nation, with a cash economy, with world-wide economic and political involvement. American Protestantism was characterized by perhaps a dozen large national denominations with representative government and with memberships drawn chiefly from the middle class. In Canada the Methodists had outstripped the Church of England numerically. But apart from French Catholic Quebec, the rest of Canada reflected the same general situation as the United States, except for the closer ties with the Empire.

The Modern Period, 1914-Present

World War I represented a decisive turning point in American history in the permanent defeat of isolationism and the reluctant acceptance of membership in the world community. Although we are too close to the history of this period to analyze it objectively, some points seem to be clear:

The metropolis: the focus of modern North America Whereas nineteenth-century North America was agricultural and rural, in the twentieth century it is urban and industrial. One-tenth of the population of the United States resides in the New York metropolitan area; half the population of the nation resides in ten great metropolitan centers. Financially and religiously, North America has developed a metropolitan culture.

The denomination: the key factor Though local congregations are strong, the high mobility rate—the average family moves once every five years—points to the denomination as the ultimate source of stability in religious organizations. Congregations continue to resent "headquarters," but financially and theologically the denomination, as a national religious organization, is the indispensable element in America Protestant church life. In the past twenty-five years the city councils of churches have grown rapidly. Some leaders—for example Dr. Henry Pitney Van Dusen, formerly President of Union Theological Seminary, and Dr. Truman Douglas of the Board of Home Missions, Congregational Christian Churches—think that the most authentic expression of New Testament Christianity is the city council of churches. In spite of this Van Dusen-Douglas view, the national denomination still seems to be the prime source of religious strength.

The Every Member Canvass is the prime stewardship technique In the late nineteenth century the typical pattern for the support of the congregation and its mission enterprises was the "subscription list." A few laymen, over a period of several months, would visit well-to-do members to solicit financial support for the year. This informal, hit-and-miss technique resulted in sporadic and ineffective support for the churches. Most missionary giving came from vigorous women's groups which conducted "benefits" of various kinds and collected "egg money" and other small sums from housewives.

During the first decade of the twentieth century Charles Ward, a YMCA secretary in Grand Rapids, Michigan, developed the "intensive campaign." This was a limitation of the time for collecting pledges to a brief period of possibly a month, and the enlistment of volunteer visitors who did the calling during this short period. Mr. Ward's technique attracted immediate attention throughout the YMCA and the philanthropic world generally. The decade 1910-1920 saw many communions adopting the "Every Member Canvass" as a standard formula.

The church version of the "intensive campaign" was relatively simple. A large number of laymen were called together during the closing weeks of the year for an evening of training and orientation as to the needs of the church. They were sent out during November or December to secure pledges from the church members for the coming year. The pledges were usually on the weekly basis and were for both local expenses and missions. The offering envelopes supplied generally were of the double-pocket variety. This plan continued in most communions until 1948, when the Presbyterian Church in the U.S.A. adopted "Planned Education" for the Every Member Canvass.

This Presbyterian refinement of the Every Member Canvass technique made use of a film strip for training the canvassers and a turnover chart for the presentation of the method and message in the home. The Presbyterian plan was further refined in 1951 by the "Baptist Sector Plan," or the "Eight-Step Every Member Canvass." The basic features of the "Sector Plan" were: (1) an analysis of the giving potential of the congregation, drawing upon techniques perfected by various professional fund-raising organizations; and (2) adequate intensive program planning. About 1955 the Presbyterian Church in the U.S. (Southern) introduced the "pre-budget canvass" in which the dollar goal was not announced in advance; instead, church members were asked to make their pledges in the light of their gratitude to God, rather than to meet the obligations of a budget.

The Every Member Canvass has now been in use in North American Churches for fifty years. The validity of the canvass has not been questioned; techniques and devices continue to evolve, with considerable flexibility in detail. However, the standard pattern of a program of information in advance, the training of visitors, the call in the home, the explanation of the

44924

work of the church, the weekly pledge, and the year-round schedule of stewardship information and missionary education, seem firmly established.

The capital funds campaign North American Protestantism makes a clear distinction between the continuing current funds and special capital funds. It is assumed that the needs of the local congregation and the world outreach program will go on forever. However, from time to time, a congregation may need to build a new parish hall or a new sanctuary, or engage in a special capital-funds campaign for a missionary project or for a denominational college or hospital. The great pioneer Charles Ward organized a professional fund-raising firm which continues to this day under the name Ward, Dreshman and Reinhardt. After 1910 hundreds of professional fund-raising firms have come into existence. Since the Protestant churches almost immediately adapted the methods of Charles Ward for the Every Member Canvass, the services of these professional fund-raising firms since 1916 have not been widely used in connection with Every Member Canvass campaigns. The one exception is that the Marts and Lundy firm assisted in developing the 1951 Baptist Sector Plan. On the other hand, the professional fund-raising firms have had great influence on the capital-funds campaigns of North American churches.

Some of the denominations had been offering professional capital-funds services as early as 1932. With results so dramatically demonstrated by the growth of the Wells Organizations, most denominations greatly amplified their services in this area so that today American Protestant denominations employ about 100 men as capital-funds directors, giving professional service and charging fees large enough to make the work largely self-supporting.

The development of unified promotion in denominational church life American Protestantism has built and now administers colleges, hospitals, homes for the aged, orphans homes, and social welfare institutions. These generally are sponsored by city or state denominational groups. Most colleges, for example, are sponsored by state or regional synod groups. During much of the nineteenth century this support came through offerings after a special speaker representing the institution appealed to a local congregation. It was expensive to send professional speakers to different congregations every Sunday. The congregations became weary of multiple appeals. Gradually, during the first part of the twentieth century, a unified national denominational benevolence program emerged. Denominational agencies merged their financial needs into a unified budget and presented them in a systematic way to the local congregation. Usually the foreign mission board was represented in the larger percentage, then followed national missions, Christian education, pensions, hospitals, and other institutions. While there was always some jockeying for position, and pushing and pulling regarding allocations, the essential principle of unified promotion became an accepted part of denominational church life. By whatever name most denominations set up departments of stewardship and promotion which prepared leaflets, booklets, and films, and trained personnel. The United Stewardship Council, organized in 1920, brought together these denominational stewardship and promotional executives into an effective group. The Department of Stewardship and Benevolence of the National Council of Churches of Christ in the U.S.A. is the successor agency to the United Stewardship Council and represents both the stewardship ideal and the practical necessity of raising several billion dollars annually.

The rediscovery of tithing   While tithing has always been advocated in North American Protestantism to some degree, the period 1945-1960 can definitely be said to mark a "rediscovery of tithing." Tithing is usually defined as giving at least 10 per cent of the worker's pay to church and charity. There are other interpretations, but this seems to fit most conditions. Most Protestant communions in the United States and Canada have a quiet but steady stream of materials promoting the idea of proportionate giving, beginning with the tithe. While tithing is a controversial topic, there has been tremendous new interest in it during the past twenty years.

The development of theology   The thirty-year period 1930-1960 has witnessed a theological "boom" in American church life. The output of theological books has increased. Stewardship has felt the impact of the new theological interest. Books by Holmes Rolston, T. A. Kantonen, Luther P. Powell, and Helge Brattgard have been well received. A major publisher has announced a "Library of Christian Stewardship" that may run to ten or twelve volumes. More than a hundred theological seminaries include some treatment of stewardship within their curricula.

Conclusion

In North America, with the separation of church and state, voluntary giving became the necessary form of church support. Churches have thrived under this pattern. Church-related colleges and social welfare institutions have fared poorly. Voluntary giving and congregational policy have been the two foci of American Protestantism. These patterns fitted the pioneer life of the eighteenth and nineteenth centuries. Whether Protestantism has an effective stewardship strategy for twentieth century industrial, urban America is still an open question. The answer may well be found in the churches' interpretation of the Gospel to modern man and their involvement in the changing world. Christian stewardship with its call to commitment of life and resources will be a necessary part in the renewal of the churches.

9

STEWARDSHIP AND MISSION
IN THE LOCAL CHURCH

Winburn T. Thomas

"A church which is not on mission, which is not at God's convenience, has ceased in any sense recognizable by the Holy Scripture to be a church." [1] The preceding chapters have indicated some of the dimensions of this mission, and have stressed stewardship of time, abilities, and resources as a means of its fulfillment. The church must begin at home, but if it remains there it is sick unto death.

Christian stewardship and Christian mission alike rest on the Biblical affirmation that God has acted to save men by giving His Son, Jesus Christ. Through His birth, life, death, and resurrection, He has demonstrated God's power to save His creation. This good news has been entrusted to Christ's church in each generation of believers to be proclaimed to the whole world.

The church exists to move in the world witnessing to the good news, and serving men as the Body of Christ. The church fulfills this responsibility as its members, nurtured and instructed, accept their ministry. As we devote ourselves and our resources to this task, we practice stewardship that the world may believe. The mission which God gives us brings with it the means to accomplish it: "All things are of God, who hath recon-

[1] *Compass*, December 1963, p. 4.

ciled us to himself by Jesus Christ, and hath given to us the ministry of reconciliation" (II Corinthians 5:18).

CONGREGATIONAL STEWARDSHIP

The "me-first" attitude of people is the major handicap of the churches in undertaking their rightful share of the world Christian mission. Far too small a portion of the members' income is contributed to the church, and the congregation in turn may absorb up to 85-90 per cent of its total income in the local program. Frequently, the benevolence allocation may be the last item in the local budget to be paid. The pastor, the officers, and the congregation need to recognize, therefore, the congregation's basic obligations as stewards when decisions are being made with respect to the church's money.

CHURCH BUILDINGS AND PROPERTY

In an effort to keep up with the Joneses, local congregations feel their facilities must be kept modern and up-to-date irrespective of the needs of the church in the world beyond. Much of the investment is in the sanctuary which is used only two or three hours weekly. Luxurious lounges, extra modern kitchens, stained-glass windows, foam-rubber cushions in the pews are the kind of extras which drain off the funds which might otherwise be used in church extension and Christian service.

Before embarking upon an expansion or improvement program the church should ask: Is this expenditure really necessary? Could the congregation be accommodated by an additional service? Could the Sunday church school attendance be cared for by a split shift? Will the facilities planned be used sufficiently to justify their cost?

Some churches, aware of their mission and contemplating an expansion program, have tithed their building budget; others have undertaken to erect a building in some missionary location before embarking on their own; others have insisted that the mission (or benevolence) pledge be increased and subscribed before embarking upon the raising of funds for the local building. Such devices are useful reminders to the local membership that theirs is not a church unto itself, but is part of a world-wide Body of Christ which is called to a ministry of witness and service.

PROGRAM BUILDING

Stewardship is also involved in program building. Many congregations look to staff expansion as a means of obtaining the persons needed to resource the church's activities, without examining its own roll of members for the needed time and capacities. The introspective character of many such programs justifies the cynical description of the Protestant minister as being a private chaplain, communally sustained. The final decisions should be made within the context of the total mission of the church, and not only the needs within the community or the church membership. For instance, if the church decides to call an extra staff person, the membership should examine the congregation's record of recruitment for church vocations. The decision to spend a given sum for local program should be evaluated in comparison to the amount contributed by the congregation for the church's work beyond the local program.

THE DIVISION OF FUNDS

Congregations, no less than individuals, should give from gratitude and not out of their surplus. The local ministry is important, but so is the total program of the church as a whole. Each local church should seek to reach its highest potential in giving to the total work of the church, setting a preliminary goal of $1 for general mission (benevolence) for every $2 raised for the local mission, then striving for a one-to-one basis when the first goal is reached.

Any appeals for funds which are not approved by the denomination as a whole should be carefully scrutinized by congregations. The church's national staff make allocations to projects which on the basis of their study appears to be the most judicious use of funds likely to be made available. These decisions are made with a view to the needs of the world, not just under the influence of a skilled speaker who presents an immediate, dramatic need. In most instances the congregation would make better use of any funds which might be available for mission by making them available to the boards and agencies of the church than by allocating money for special appeals made outside the budget.

A YEAR-ROUND PROGRAM OF MISSION INVOLVEMENT

Each Christian is called to be a steward to fulfill the mission God initiated through Christ, whom He gave to the world for its redemption. Christ has entrusted to His church the good news to be proclaimed to all the world, and the chosen people of God are so to incarnate Christ's love that the world may believe in God who sent Christ. The Christian, then, has been entrusted with a life with certain gifts and material resources which he is charged by God to use as a steward. He practices stewardship that Christ's mission may be proclaimed; the church acts as a receiving and distribution center for the body of Christian stewards who comprise the church. Stewardship involves the expenditure of self, represented by money, so that the giving of money is a valid expression of stewardship.

Stewardship and mission cannot be disposed of by an annual kick-off sermon preceding the Every Member Canvass or Stewardship Campaign, or by inviting in a missionary to the Indians to speak of "his work." Stewardship and mission should infuse every sermon, address, and church activity. If they are integral to the congregation's year-round program, then the families of the church will become so involved in the total outreach and purpose of the church that the pledging to the annual budget will be but an incident in the calendar—just one of the many activities whereby they show their gratitude for what God has done and is doing for them.

The pastor and officers of the church will then plan a year-round program of preaching, education, and activities designed to educate and involve the members individually and as families in stewardship for the mission of the church. Since the time, the abilities, as well as the money of the church community must be committed for this purpose, this section is devoted to suggesting ways and means, recognizing that each congregation must consider local factors that will require adaptations.

Every sermon, every church school class, and every special event should be so designed as to remind the people that the church exists to fulfill its mission.

1. The pastor should make use of illustrative material in his sermons which points up the Christian responsibility for witnessing in and serving the world which, despite its lost state, is the objective of God's love. The *religion* section of weekly news magazines frequently supplies such materials. Pulpit and offertory prayers, children's sermons, and talks to church groups also should be saturated with the theme of the church's mission. The morning liturgy in some churches includes "The Pastor's Minute" in which the minister may describe a mission project, recount an incident, or expound on a subject otherwise foreign to the planned sermon of the day.

2. Missionaries, overseas nationals, settlement house workers, college presidents, and other workers from the church's frontiers should be invited to preach, speak, and spend time within the congregation.

3. A continuing relationship with persons or projects beyond the local parish should be established and cultivated by a regular exchange of letters, visits, pictures, sound-tapes, etc. The relationship may or may not have a price tag attached depending upon the over-all policy of the denominational body.

4. Films, film strips, and tapes which depict and personalize the church's engagement in mission should be scheduled periodically for the various events which comprise the church's calendar. A concentration of this may be planned, extending over an entire week.

5. Descriptive leaflets, brochures, and other mission interpretative literature should be mailed out periodically to church members, and included in the literature racks.

6. Visits of church groups should be arranged to

nearby church colleges, university foundations, theological seminaries, home missions projects, and other expressions of the church's missionary concern.

7. A series of "Church Family Nights" should be scheduled for the study of the materials provided for the denomination's annual mission by the minister or some church layman; the themes may be illustrated by motion pictures, or a representative of the area under study may be invited to speak about the subject.

8. The Sunday bulletin should carry short items, facts, reports of events illustrating the work of the church around the world.

9. The training of new members should include a review of the concept of mission, an account of how the church is engaged in fulfilling Christ's mission in the world, and a challenge to the new members to engage in the mission task.

10. A room in the church or a section of the church parlor should be set aside for displays of mission materials, book exhibits, a world map, and other materials illustrating the mission of the church and the challenge of the world situation. Assign responsibility to different groups within the church to arrange the exhibit periodically. The map, for instance, could carry streamers leading from the local church itself to points where its denomination has a stake in the missionary enterprise, to missonaries and projects to which the congregation is related, to tension spots in the world, etc.

11. Keep up with the world events in the church. Assign to individuals, squads of individual members, or to separate church groups the responsibility for keeping abreast of the world. Assignments could be made to those lands where missionaries related to the congregation are at work, to the lands where the denomination is engaged in mission, to the major continents, or to each of the nations of the world. As these nations become featured in the news, arrange for the "expert" in the church to comment on the

facts and meaning of the crisis, and to indicate the significance of the situation for the church. This report might be made during the "Pastor's Minute" before special groups meeting in the church.

12. Resettle a refugee family in the community, arranging a home, finding employment for the head of the household, and minister to the family until the members have found their places.

13. Provide hospitality for foreign students and trainees, and for military personnel who may be located near the town or city where the church is located.

14. Provide a ministry, and show hospitality and friendliness to the seasonal migrants who may be working adjacent to the area where the church is located.

15. Work out a relationship to a settlement house, an inner city mission, a new church development project, or a church consisting of a minority race, where volunteers can participate in the ministry.

16. Organize the church members into teams according to the sections of the town or city in which they reside, to extend the work of the church to all needful situations in their neighborhoods, such as calling on the sick, aiding the poor, dealing with tension situations, calling on newcomers, etc.

17. Organize a study group for church members and/or others in the community who may be planning a visit overseas, or who may be assigned overseas, to orient them with respect to overseas living, working with the churches abroad, etc.

18. Recruit candidates for church vocations, counsel concerning professional training, help establish contacts with the proper board or agency of the church which makes appointments, trains, etc.

These suggestions are but samples of the ways in which the church can seek to fulfill its part of the total world mission. The heresy of Protestantism is that people are invited *to* church. Rather, the church should be so involved with the world that its members are challenged and trained to go out as the church to minister, to witness, and to serve where men live.

These activities presuppose a commitment on the part of the membership, for no pastor can do all these things, nor even train the membership of the church to do them. The local operation, therefore, must be so organized that responsibilities for training and doing are carried by the laymen and laywomen who also are ministers, endowed with certain gifts.

The responsible governing body of the church, therefore, should organize a committee charged with mission, with assignments within the membership for particular aspects of the task which are relevant to the capacities and time of the persons involved.

FINANCIAL STEWARDSHIP

"Stewardship" has become an objectionable term in parts of the church because of its identification with money-raising. As the preceding articles have evidenced, an interpretation which limits the term to budget-raising does violence to its Biblical basis. The term must be used in its fullness, and the whole church life infused with its larger and deeper meanings.

Yet, let not this inclusive exposition blind us to the fact that *money* is involved. For modern man money is stored work: it is the basis of his livelihood. He exchanges it for most of the goods and services upon which his physical life is based. It is not a dirty term to be eschewed in church. Money too belongs to God, and should be used by His servants to advance Christ's mission. Stewardship education, therefore, includes instruction in the giving of money, which in its own way is a form of Christian witness and service.

The organization of a congregation to give is, therefore, integral to its total work and program. The plans must be structured, responsibilities must be assigned, and the work accomplished in this area, even with respect to other aspects of the church's life and work. Paul did not regard money as being secondary in the Kingdom's work. Writing to the Corinthians, following his exposition of the spiritual body, he says:

Therefore, my beloved brethren, be steadfast, immovable, always abounding in the work of the Lord, knowing that in the Lord your labor is not in vain.

Now concerning the contributions for the saints . . . (I Corinthians 15:58-16:1).

QUESTIONABLE STEWARDSHIP METHODS AND ARGUMENTS

God needs, not so much the money of the member, as he needs the person. Giving is a worshipful act of gratitude for what God has done and is doing for us through Christ. The funds so handled by the church are for purposes of fulfilling Christ's mission. There is no necessary correlation between the amount of money and what is accomplished. The amount contributed is important in that it is an index of the steward's gratitude and commitment.

The raising of funds through commercial ventures debases the very mission for which the church exists. Bazaars, raffles, bake sales, money-raising meals and shows become substitutes for stewardship, and become substitutes for the very mission activity which the church alone can do.

Likewise objectionable are civic arguments, that a church is good for a community; that giving merits respect, since the giver should not let his right hand know what his left hand does; that the church is a bulwark against Communism; or that a person should match what his neighbor has given. The church's mission is to be supported by the stewardship of its members, and the basis for stewardship is Biblical, not pragmatic.

CONCLUSION

"With his sure sense of history, he would have appreciated the fact that his own niche in history will be made not by the number or variety of places bearing his name nor by the marble buildings erected in his honor, but by the effect of his life . . ." Thus *The New York Times* (December 29, 1963) commented upon the rededication of airports, towns, and bridges in memory of the late President John F. Kennedy. The editor quoted President Lyndon B. Johnson as saying, ". . . we honor him best by honoring the purposes which he championed during his life—by pressing on his fight for a just and peaceful world, in which all peoples in all lands may look forward to lives of freedom and opportunity and hope for themselves and their children. Let such a world be his monument."

The Christian church appears to have lost sight of this fact in the way it seeks to honor its Founder and its Lord. His followers in the U.S.A. invest one billion dollars annually in new palaces and marble buildings bearing His name, but are reluctant to proclaim the good news of His death and resurrection, or to press His mission which was for "all peoples in all lands." The conclusion of the editorial is equally Biblical and relevant to our point, "In His life (He) shed light all around the world. In His death (and resurrection) that light will live on in the hearts of men, which is the only place where it can never be extinguished."